T.

Unearthing Lost Resurrection Stories

Other Books By Tyler

Stories of The Supernatural
How To Raise The Dead
The Coming
The UnRedeemed

Would you give our book a stellar Amazon
review? Thank you!

First Printing, 2016

PO Box 1392
Shelton, WA 98584

www.OneGlance.org

"Go back and report to John what you have seen
and heard: The blind receive sight,
the lame walk,
those who have leprosy are cleansed,
the deaf hear, **the dead are raised**,
and the good news is proclaimed to the poor."
-Jesus, Luke 7:22

CONTENTS

INTRODUCTION

For some people resurrection is a murky topic, wrought with unsettling ideas stemming from misguided and sometimes completely unbiblical beliefs. This happens when someone's idea of resurrection is shaped more by Hollywood than by the truth found in scripture. The beauty of resurrection will assuredly elude a person if they are fearful of it, much like God Himself. The truth is that dead raising is incredibly wonderful and beautiful, full of compassion and love.

And just as God is love, resurrection is first and foremost about love. This point is commonly overshadowed when people grapple with the topic of dead raising. But think about it: With resurrection, at a family's lowest point, God swoops in and restores their loved one's life. All of their grief, all of their sadness, all of the confusion and questions that death causes a person to experience is suddenly erased. When heaven manifests on earth, "He wipes away every tear" (Rev. 21:4).

Resurrection is the apex manifestation of gentleness, kindness, and heartfelt empathy. It is the restoration of family. In fact, aside from the cross, there are few things in the Bible more endowed with compassion and love than a child or parent being raised back to life from the dead and being handed back to their family. If we can focus on the inherent, overflowing compassion found within resurrection, the stigma this topic has carried will be replaced by an understanding of its beauty.

What is more, resurrection is not merely an event or a miracle but God's very character. In John 11:25 Christ declared, "I am the resurrection and the life". Abundant life is an inescapable facet of His personality. Resurrection is who He is. The beauty of resurrection is that it reveals to us that He cannot help but bring life to any situation that He is invited into. God is the embodiment of resurrection. The carrier of life, He raises anything back to life that has died when He is near. Everything is sustained by Him, breath by breath.

Additionally, the very validity of Christianity hinges upon the reality that one Man was raised from the dead. If Christ was not raised then everything even remotely associated with Christianity is mistaken. What a glorious reality! Even the mere topic of resurrection leaves us with no choice to leap into the mysterious realm of wonder and faith. In 1 Corinthians 15:12-17 Paul says it like this:

"But if it is preached that Christ has been raised from the dead, how can some of you say that there is no resurrection of the dead? If there is no resurrection of the dead, then not even Christ has been raised. And if Christ has not been raised, our preaching is useless and so is your faith. More than that, we are then found to be false witnesses about God, for we have testified about God that he raised Christ from the dead. But he did not raise him if in fact the dead are not raised. For if the dead are not raised, then Christ has not been raised either. And if Christ has not been raised, your faith is futile; you are still in your sins."

The truth is that Lazarus really was called forth from the grave, women actually did receive back their dead, and Christ was raised. Everything you have heard is true! These are not myths, legends, tall tales, or stories of fiction. In fact, according to Romans 10:9, one cannot call themselves a "Christian" without inherently believing that Christ physically died and was physically raised back to life.

"...if you confess with your mouth, 'Jesus is Lord', and believe in your heart that God has raised him from the dead, you will be saved."

This book will build your faith through the overwhelmingly abundant occurrences of the deceased being resurrected to life throughout history. The testimonies are organized chronologically so that the reader can see that since Christ gave the commandment to "raise the dead" (Matthew 10:8), He has been consistent and faithful in backing up those that step out and obey Him. God wouldn't tell us to do something that He wouldn't anoint to fulfill. Also, the last chapter is a recounting of the resurrections recorded in the Bible, some rarely taught on or even acknowledged.

The testimonies in this book come from primarily Catholic sources. While I do not regard myself as Catholic, there is much life to be had through the testimonies of the Catholic men and women that have gone before us. There is a tremendous plethora of testimonies, wisdom, and experience to feast upon that our Catholic brothers and sisters have stored up, and it has gone largely ignored, untapped, and disregarded by Protestants. Catholicism has been around for more than 1800 years; Protestantism has been around for only about 500 years. As Protestants, we are the new kid on the block. When we assume that we have nothing to learn from our elder brother, the Catholic church, we instantly cut ourselves off from the wealth of testimonies stored up for us over those first 1500 years of church history prior to Luther and the Reformation. Don't you want to know of God's faithfulness and power through His working of miracles during that enormous amount of time? I did. The result is this book. The stories I came across astounded me; they will astound you as well.

It is always wisdom to listen to and receive from those that have gone before us, honoring their lives and soaking up their wisdom, even if we don't wholeheartedly agree with them theologically. In everything, even in Protestant settings, we are encouraged by God to eat the meat and spit out the bones so that our knowledge, faith, and love can be expounded upon to the greatest degree, but we are never encouraged in scripture to throw the baby out with the bath water. Solomon ended badly but God didn't take his writings out of the Bible. David was a murderer and adulterer but God didn't erase his life from history because he made mistakes. I am not Catholic but I cannot disregard what God has done in the past because of Catholic practices and beliefs that I do not participate in.

There are many resurrections that occurred throughout history that are not included in this book. Instead of recounting every resurrection miracle that has ever happened, my hope for this book would be to convey the sheer unchangeableness of God pertaining to resurrection by looking at His faithfulness throughout history. The outcome of such faithfulness on God's behalf has a way of instilling faith into us, thus resulting in each of us also fulfilling the wonder of Matthew 10:8 to "… raise the dead…"

As I researched this book a wonderful problem evolved; too many resurrection testimonies were uncovered. There were numerous times when a mother brought a small child to a monk or priest and they were restored to life. Each story is beautiful and worshipful, but for the sake of brevity, not every testimony that was discovered can be included in this book. Thus, the accounts that may test the limits of our faith will rest upon these pages.

Have your ever heard a testimony that simply sounded unbelievable? I have personally seen God do incredible miracles but nonetheless, time and time again as I researched this book I came across stories that revealed to me the limits I have on God's miracle-working power. These limits are usually hidden and unconscious, and I have found that I only become aware of them when something shining so brightly of another Kingdom illuminates my blind spots of unbelief. I know when this process of growing in faith or being stretched is taking place in me because of a few steps that I go through. You may relate.

First, I feel uncomfortable. When I hear or read an unbelievable testimony it gives me the same feeling as if a stranger knocked on the door to my house and upon opening the door, joyfully came inside without invitation and informed me that they will be staying for an undetermined amount of time. Discomfort is a good word for this first phase. Second, I argue. I argue with the story and sometimes unknowingly deny it or undermine it. If a person gets past this hump it is all downhill from there but sometimes this is as far as people get. I know when I haven't allowed a testimony to build my faith and encourage me because I relate to it in a way that is equivalent to a shrug. I say things in a monotone voice like, "Oh sure, I totally believe God could do something like that. Of course!" In essence, that is me saying that I do not believe that God did do something like that. My loss. Third, I let go of my pride and accept the story's possibility. It isn't that hard...but I have to choose to be like a child that doesn't act like they know everything... unlike an adult. Forth, I remember that there are impossible claims made in scripture. Completely impossible. And I believe scripture to be true, unequivocally. Thus the story must transition from possible to plausible in my heart, despite how impossible it is in the natural, simply because scripture says impossible things happened. The heart of the situation isn't who was involved or what supposedly happened or how reliable the source is that made the claim but if God is in fact capable of doing the impossible. Lastly, once I have eaten enough truth to partially deflate my unbelief, I finally begin to get excited. I imagine the scenario in my head and begin to feel the awe, beauty, relief, power, and joy of the situation. I actually start to believe.

I think you will find that reading this book is akin to uncovering a chest of treasure in your backyard that was buried by time: It was always there and always possessed incredible value; It just needed to be uncovered. The past has a way of getting lost and covered up if we do not seek it out. You have sought it out by picking up this book, and now you shall find.

Since Christ was raised from the dead and God does not change (Mal. 3:6, Heb. 13:8), then it stands to reason that God has been raising the dead, is raising the dead, and will continue to raise the dead. He is the same yesterday, today, and forever. Thus, the dead are raised.

-Tyler G. Johnson

FOREWORD

History is full of reformers who in their era saw what needed to be changed, and with deep passion and conviction created change. I believe Tyler Johnson to be one of these reformers. His books, words, and life challenge and encourage us to believe that the fundamental teaching of Christ to raise the dead... never died.

Resurrection from the dead is a central and distinguishing truth of the Gospel of Jesus Christ. When Christ gave up His spirit on the cross, many people walked out of their tombs, raised from the dead. The Bible records this event as if it is the new normal. Since His resurrection, there have been more resurrections from the dead than at any other time previously recorded in human history. Though each of these have eyewitness accounts by family members and friends, still a skeptical mind exists that would seek to discredit them as improbable or fictional tales. There are many logical arguments to discredit these accounts, but each are fueled by the same rhetoric that even disputes the resurrection of Jesus. Simply put, without faith it is impossible to believe that someone dead would come back to life! This makes pursuing resurrection from the dead risky business, for not only is it foundational to the Gospel, but it is also the most controversial.

Whether it is an anti-God belief system, a competitively religious mindset, or attempts by some scholars to isolate resurrections strictly to a biblical narrative, history is replete with book burnings and other acts that would seek to eradicate this truth from our Christian heritage.

Only God knows how many records of resurrections throughout history have been lost, destroyed, or are hidden... and awaiting discovery. In this book you will read many resurrection accounts that have been hidden, but thanks to Tyler will not be forgotten.

To the average person, the thought of "radical believers" going about finding dead people to pray back to life is a lot to handle! The simple truth is this: Jesus never intended dead raising to be limited to radical believers.... just being a believer is all it takes to qualify! As Tyler often points out, Jesus told his followers to raise the dead. To Jesus (and remember, He is our founder), raising the dead and healing the sick are a natural response to following Him. These are powerful acts of His compassion and this same Christ-like compassion lives deep within every believer.

In this day, the thought of raising someone from the dead is quite intimidating to modern believers — and Tyler believes this needs to change. His passion is to help the believer move beyond the restrictive thinking of "God only did miracles in the biblical past," to Jesus Christ is the same yesterday, today and forever (Heb 13:8). What God did in ages past, He will do today. His miracle-working-power transcends the barriers of time and space! Remember, the same Spirit that raised Christ from the dead, lives in us and causes our mortal bodies to come to life (Rom 8:11). We are carriers of resurrection life!

Those of us who know Tyler Johnson count ourselves blessed. He is genuine, passionate, and honest in communicating the goodness of God. My wife and I both love his books and use *How to Raise the Dead* as a textbook at our Faith Supernatural School of Ministry. Like other reformers, he has decided that doubting minds should not be commonplace in the Church of the Living God. He has boldly determined "to take captive every argument that opposes the knowledge of the supernatural, dead-raising God, and cause it to obey Christ" (2 Cor 10:4, 5). Tyler is taking thoughts captive by writing, speaking, and living a supernatural life. He also leads Dead Raising Teams around the world who are actively pursuing the miraculous and raising the dead. My wife Lin and I have come to know and love Tyler. We love how he thinks and teaches on the goodness of God—and how he stretches us to live expectantly for the miraculous! Tyler is an inspiration to our life and ministry. In just a three-year period alone, our Dead Raising Team has prayed for multiple dead in which six have come back to life! At scenes of accidents, in morgues, hospitals, or wherever the dead are found—our people hold to the belief that all things are possible. Some have come back, others haven't, but our course is not altered. Jesus said we could raise the dead, and we believe that His Spirit lives in us to accomplish this task.

If you are a believer and think dead-raising is limited to the Bible, or think that it is beyond your everyday "gifting"... turn the page and prepare to have your faith ignited!

Daryl Nicolet
Senior Leader & Founder
Faith Worship Center
Pepperell, Massachusetts
FaithWorship.org

Chapter One
(270AD-550AD)

Biblical Accounts
(971BC-90AD)

It goes without saying that the most foundational resurrections are the accounts recorded in scripture, the one having the greatest significance and impact being Christ's own victory over death. Those gloriously bewildering accounts are covered from a firsthand perspective in the last chapter of this book. The first hand perspective adds an element of reality and raw newness to stories that we all too easily skim over, putting us in the shoes of those that witnessed these resurrections actually taking place. The biblical accounts have been placed at the end of the book because most readers are already aware of them and starting this book with accounts that are largely unknown to most people took priority. Hence, let us pick up with an incredible account of resurrection that took place not long after the last book of the Bible was written with a man named Nicolas from the ancient city of Myra, in present-day Turkey.

·

"No doctrine of the Christian faith
is so vehemently and so obstinately opposed
as the doctrine of the resurrection of the flesh."
-Augustine, 396AD

Nicholas of Myra
(270AD-343AD)

Nicholas of Myra, also commonly referred to as Saint Nic, is well known for his acts of generosity but the more miraculous aspects of his life have been whittled away by time. Everyone is familiar with Santa and his reindeer, but few people know that Mr. Christmas actually raised the dead! What follows is one of the most incredible testimonies from Nic's life.

Nicholas lived in an era of consistent famine. Once when he was traveling in an area especially afflicted by famine, Nic had a vision of an innkeeper that was running short on meat to serve to the people staying at his establishment. In the vision, the innkeeper went out and kidnapped three small boys and brought them back to his inn. He chopped up their bodies with an axe, then put the body parts in a pickling barrel, filling it with brine in an attempt to cure the meat, with the plans to serve it to his guests once it was ready.

Nicholas came out of prayer, stood to his feet, and went into town with the motive of finding the inn that he had seen in his vision. After a short while of searching, he came upon the inn. He walked inside and confronted the innkeeper, communicating that he knew what the man had done. White as a sheet, the innkeeper is said to have taken Nicholas downstairs to the location of the pickling barrel. Nicholas prayed over the barrel and then ordered the innkeeper to open it. Upon the barrel being opened, three little boys crawled out of the pickling juice completely restored, raised from the dead.

What a wonderful account of God's love. Think of the grief that God saved the mothers of these children. Imagine how amazing it would have been to see those little boys crawl out of that liquid! "With God all things are possible." Stories like these cause a person to ask if they really believe that statement, don't they? God is the creator of the universe; surely if He made man from dust to begin with, He can put a human body back together. "Nothing is impossible with God." If nothing is impossible with God, then that means that all limitations are determined by us. If we will only believe, any kind of impossibility becomes possible.

There is a well known song that is sung about Santa Claus during the Christmas season that goes like this: "He knows when you are sleeping, He knows when you're awake. He knows if you've been bad or good, so be good for goodness sake." Oddly enough, this pseudo omniscience attributed to Santa actually stems from the story of the children and the barrel in the life of St. Nic. "He knows if you've been bad...." was not intended to be a performance-based threat given to children in an attempt to curb bad behavior, but alluded to the word of knowledge that Nic got pertaining to the innkeeper. The warning in this song wasn't originally meant to be directed towards children, but to those that would harm children. In this light, the lyrics in the song are reminiscent of Jesus' words, "If anyone causes one of these little ones to stumble, it would be better for them if..."

We have misunderstood the moral of this well-known song largely because we lost the story that originally went along with it. This song wasn't intended to scare kids into acting right, but rightly warn those that would do harm to children. The result of losing the original context of the song is that we have sculpted a performance based mentality around Christmas (and Santa) rather than a holiday where we remember that it is not our performance that qualifies us for the good things that God gives us but the fact that Christ's performance in coming as a little baby to the earth and eventually dying for us is what has already qualified us for the good things that God gives us. It could be argued that this song isn't about stockings full of coal but a barrel full of resurrected kids.

There are paintings and sculptures of Nicholas and the three boys in churches all over the world, some dating back to the Middle Ages. Even recently, around the Christmas season, Godiva Chocolate produced a chocolate figure of St. Nicholas that had three boys in a pickling barrel at his feet. You can still find the molds available for purchase online that the chocolate would be poured into to make the statues. With dead raising being something that has been considered a fringe topic for 2,000 years, it is ironic that some of our major national holidays actually celebrate the lives of people that raised the dead. Christmas is such a holiday. Next time you are opening presents on Christmas, remember St. Nicholas and the three boys. Remember that while Christmas is about the Prince of Peace making His earthly debut, it is also about His victory over death.

A more well known story is one about St. Nic and the dowries of the three daughters, which further connects Nic to the modern idea of Santa. The story goes like this: There was a poor father with three daughters. His daughters needed to be married off, but the dad did not have the money to pay the dowry to the men that would marry them. Because the father didn't know what to do and couldn't sustain supporting the three women, he entertained selling the women into slavery. St. Nic somehow caught on to what was going on, and dropped enough money through the window of the family's house for one daughter's dowry to be paid. The father gladly gave her away to be married, but still had the issue of paying for the other two daughter's dowries. Nic dropped a bag of money through their window again, resulting in the second daughter being married off. Now though, the father was curious how this money was ending up on the floor of his house, so he closed off the windows to his house in the hope that he would get an opportunity to thank whoever was giving such generous gifts. Nic came once again with another bag of money, but finding all the windows locked, climbed on the roof and dropped the bag of money through the chimney, avoiding any attention he would get if he was found out. Does this remind you of anyone that we talk about in December? As you can see, Santa stems from St. Nicholas. While Santa is fictitious, St. Nicholas was a very real person.

Nicholas was known to have a special love and compassion towards children. There are different testimonies backing this, such as an account of two children that were burned up in a house fire. Nic prayed over their burned bodies and they were restored to life. Nicholas raised children that had drowned, raised a man that had been crushed by the mast of a ship, and much more. How on earth have we gone so long not knowing these testimonies when year after year we celebrate Christmas? It is a fantastic thing when God unearths things that have been hidden for so long, right under our nose all along.

Martin of Tours
(316AD-397AD)

Martin was born in what is now Hungry, lived his youth out in Italy, and dwelt in France for most of his adult life. He is credited with raising the dead at least three times.

While on a trip away from the monastery, a fellow monk that was one of Martin's friends became sick and died. Upon his return to the monastery three days later, Martin found the other monks in grief as they prepared his body for burial. Martin is said to have started weeping over the death of his friend, then told the rest of the monks to leave the cell where the body was located. Martin then proceeded to lock the door and pray in private for his friend's resurrection. After two hours, the man's arms began to move. Not long after that, the half man opened his eyes, then blinked rapidly at the light. Martin unlocked the door as he began praising God with shouts, which caused the other monks to come into the room, where they found their fellow companion completely restored from death.

Later, the monk that had died recounted what happened to him when he was dead. Stripped of his body, he had been led before some sort of judge where he was sentenced to go with an "unsavory" group of people to a region of darkness. Just before they were going to leave, two angels brought word to the judge that this man was the person that Martin was praying for. The man was released and the angels then led him back, where he was to be restored to Martin and given his life back.

We have to remember that people's experiences are

interpreted through the grid of understanding that they have at the time of the experience. Because of this, we have to take any experience someone has with a grain of salt. When reading this monk's account of what happened when he died, most of us would assume the judge was God. Yet, God would be aware of who this man was and that Martin was praying for him; God would not need angels to inform him of any information. The enemy is also a judge of men. The enemy is called, "the accuser of the brethren", and judges men when he has the legal right to do so because of sin. The enemy has no authority, but when sin enters the picture, he is given the legal right to steal, kill, and destroy (John 10:10). The judgment of the enemy looks like using the law to legally condemn us of our sin. The enemy seeks not to bring life through judgment (as God does), but death. The devil enjoys issuing death sentences. Meanwhile, God is still a judge but His judgments are exceedingly beautiful and gracious; the justice of God was most clearly displayed by Jesus volunteering to die on a tree in our stead. Seems unfair, but that is God's version of justice; it is gloriously unfair in that we don't get what we deserve, He does. Such is the justice of God.

Thus, in this story the man was headed into hell and through Martin's prayers God sent His angels to save him. God always wills for men to not perish, but have everlasting life!

The second testimony of resurrection in the life of Martin happened not long after the first story. Martin was walking across the property of a high-ranking official named Lupicinus when he heard the sounds of grief from a house nearby. Upon entering the house to inspect what was causing the wailing, Martin found numerous people looking upon the body of a slave that had committed suicide by hanging himself.

Martin cut the body down and began praying over body. It was not long before, in front of those grieving, the slave's eyes opened. The man then grasped Martin's hand and stood up. With everyone watching, jaws on the floor, the young man walked with Martin to another room in the house.

The reasons why not to pray for the dead to be raised are many. All are misled, regardless of however plausible, because the one reason to pray for the dead to be raised trumps all; Jesus told us to do it. Sometimes people disregard resurrection prayer if the cause of death is suicide. We don't know every detail of how things work on the other side, but we do know what we are supposed to do on this side: "raise the dead." Let's not let what we don't know take precedence over what we do know. It has been clearly communicated to us by Christ in Matthew 10:8 that we are to be people that embrace the victory Christ already afflicted upon death and be givers of Life everywhere we go.

The third raising of Martin's life is exceedingly beautiful. Martin was walking to a large town that was some distance away. While crossing a large plain he saw a huge group of pagans headed in his direction. As he drew near to their multitudes, his heart began to cry out to God for these people to know the love of Christ. Just then a woman broke through the crowd and thrust a dead baby into his arms. Weeping, she looked Martin in the eyes and said, "We know you are God's friend. Give me back my son. He is my only son."

Everyone in the crowd went quiet, and the pressure was on. Yet, Martin knew that God would not let him down, especially with the salvation of all of the people hanging in the balance. Martin knelt down with the child and began to pray. The atmosphere was ripe with anticipation. Martin soon rose to his feet, and handed the restored child back to the mother in view of everyone present. It is said that because of witnessing something that was so clearly a miracle from God, the entire mass of people threw themselves at Martin's feet, asking how to give themselves to Christ. Martin led the people in prayer to receive Jesus, and the entire throng gave themselves to Christ.

Kieran of Saigher
(352AD-540AD)

Kieran was born in Ireland, on the southern island of Clear. Even the druid Magi in his mother's community recognized his destiny and calling when he was born, and they correctly foretold of the virtue and fame that Kieran would walk in during his life.

Kieran, being born into an intense era of paganism, did not come to much knowledge of Christ until he travelled to Rome at the age of thirty. After twenty years of prayer and studying scripture he was ordained and made his way back to his homeland. On his way he met Patrick of Ardmachia, who is the covered more in depth later.

The earliest account of Kieran raising the dead took place near the monastery that Kieran had established near present day Kilkenny. A man of great wealth named Fintan brought his dead son to Kieran with the hope that Kieran's God would have the power to raise the dead. Kieran prayed over the boy, named Leoghaire, and fulfilled the hopes of the father through him being raised. The young man lived for a very long time, and Fintan gave Kieran the nearby village of Rathfera to him as a token of his gratitude.

On another occasion, a king named Aengus that knew of Kieran's ability to work wonders came to him and asked him if he could prophetically tell him where his missing harpists were. Aengus had been expecting them for quite some time but they had not shown up and he was concerned for their safety. Kieran consulted the Lord and was made aware that the harpists had been ambushed and killed near a lake, their bodies thrown in, and their harps hung on the trees that lined the lake. When the king heard of what had happened, he asked Kieran to accompany him to the lake. They arrived at the lake and both began to fast and pray. After they had fasted and prayed all day, the waters of the lake drew back and revealed the bodies of the harpists. Kieran commanded them to rise, and coming out of what seemed like a deep sleep, they took their harps out of the trees and began to play music for the king and Kieran.

Another time, the chief of Aengus along with some of his men were ambushed on the banks of the river Brosnach. All were killed. Kieran heard of the tragedy and, wanting to ensure that the bodies were given a proper burial rather than eaten by wild animals, made his way to the place with a large cart in hopes to transport the bodies back to a more respectful burial spot. Once he arrived however, Kieran quickly gathered that the cart he had brought was not big enough to accommodate all of the bodies, so he cried out that in the name of Christ all those who were killed should arise and follow him. They did so, and each one became a monk under Kieran.

Kieran once raised a woman named Eathylla after she died from a bad fall. Eathylla had been dead for three days when Kieran intervened through prayer. Another time, Kieran raised a man named Cronan after seven days in the place of death. Cronan had been killed by a Munster officer, and when Kieran discovered this news, though it was a full week later, Kieran was undeterred and prayed in faith. Cronan was raised to complete health.

Heroes are people that step out where others are unwilling to go and pave the way for others to follow by risking their lives, reputations, and comfort. Kieran was one of those heroes, a person that kings could depend on to follow through…a person the King could depend on. What an honor it will be to meet him one day.

Patrick of Ardmachia
(389AD-461AD)

While some drink green beer and look for rainbows and leprechauns on St. Patrick's Day, others remember the real reasons why the world celebrates the life of this man. Not only did Patrick's humble beginnings in ministry start with his capture into slavery, consequential escape, then call from God back into the very land where he was taken into slavery (Ireland), but regularly signs and wonders followed him, including resurrections of every sort. We aren't sure exactly how many people Patrick raised as some sources claim as many as one hundred, but it was likely at least thirty-nine.

Once there was a pregnant woman named Fidelina that was in labor. For unknown reasons, while in childbirth, she died. Patrick was nearby, and a friend of Fidelina brought the body of the woman to Patrick. Patrick prayed for the woman and she was brought back to life. In addition, not long after she was raised, she gave birth a healthy baby! The account says that a "multitude" of people witnessed this woman's death and resurrection, and that the entire assembly of people gave their hearts to God as a result. In addition, not long after God brought this woman back, another woman died in childbirth and was also raised, also giving birth to a healthy baby. Breakthrough gives way to it being repeated.

"The testimony of Jesus is the spirit of prophecy." – Rev. 19:10

That is why it is good to have testimonies constantly

on our lips. It sets a standard for every conversation and is the equivalent of throwing seed everywhere you go. Everywhere a testimony is received, it plants the seed for the same miracle to grow up in the life of the hearer. Testimony is a form of prophecy. Don't hold back. Tell everyone what Jesus has done!

Another time there was a man whose son was trampled and part of his body eaten by pigs. The father went to Patrick and stricken with grief, fell at his feet asking for Patrick to work a miracle. Patrick went to one of his disciples named Malachia and told him to go raise the boy. Malachia replied, "Who is the man that may replace the bones which are broken in pieces, renew the nerves, and restore the flesh, recall the spirit to the body, and the life to the dead corpse? I will not endeavor it, nor will I with such rashness tempt the Lord, nor essay a work which I cannot finish." Patrick responded, "Hast thou not read the promise of the Lord? If you ask from my Father in my name, He will grant it unto you. And again, If you have faith, though but as a grain of mustard seed, ye shall say unto this mountain, move thou hence, and cast thyself into the sea, and it shall be done."

Then Patrick went to two bishops and asked them to raise the boy. Just like any good leader, more than just working a miracle, Patrick wanted to use the situation as an opportunity to train someone up. The bishops wisely listened, and went and prayed for the boy. The torn and mangled body of the boy was not only restored to life when they prayed, but the youthful health and strength that he had before being trampled. In other words, he didn't just get raised...he sprang up in the abundance of life. A nearby prince gave his heart to the Lord as a result, along with all of his household and the people he ruled over. Amazing.

It is refreshing that this testimony includes that the first disciple turned down Patrick when he told them to go pray for the child. It is a lesson for us. Simply said, the man was scared. His unbelief resulted in fear and hesitancy, even coming to the conclusion that it was sin to pray for the child to come back to life.

Countless times the DRT has encountered such thinking. Instead of taking the words of Christ at their face value, people complicate things. Fear and unbelief are very complicated, but faith and love are exceedingly simple. It is God's desire that we have a simplicity about our faith like a child, keeping wonder and beauty at the forefront of our thinking rather than getting bogged down by intellectual arguments that stem from fear. Love casts out fear and makes us exceedingly bold.

Another time when Patrick was in the northern part of Ireland, a king brought fourteen thousand men to learn from him. Soon the multitude was hungry. All that was nearby was a milk cow that a man named Triamus owned. Patrick asked if the man was willing to give the cow to be slain so that the people could eat. Triamus gave permission, and Patrick began thanking God in prayer for the cow. When he started praying, two stags came out from the woods on one side of them, while two boars came out of the woods on the other side of them. The animals calmly walked up to Patrick's side and sat down. The animals were prepared, everyone ate their fill, and the leftovers were abundant. The next day Triamus found a cow in his field that looked exactly like the one that he had given to Patrick to be killed, but it was alive and well, ready to continue to give him the milk he needed. It isn't known if Patrick raised it back to life or not, but it isn't out of the question.

Having the ability to work miracles quite consistently, Patrick was called upon by kings a number of times. The first time this happened was when a king named Echu was on his deathbed from a serious illness. Echu knew he was going to die, so he sent a messenger to get Patrick. He then gave the orders that when he died, he would not be buried until Patrick had prayed and done all that he felt God was leading him to do. The king did die, and just as he had ordered, was left out and not buried. Patrick arrived a day later, mourned over the king, then prayed and the king was raised to life. Echu received Jesus not long after that. Beautiful.

Another story including a king took place in the largest city in Ireland called Athcliath at the time, and is one of the most well documented resurrections in the life of Patrick.

The story starts with St. Patrick ministering at the home of a woman who didn't have access to fresh water. Patrick is said to have struck the ground and a fountain of fresh, clear water sprung up where he had hit the ground, not unlike Moses. Meanwhile, a mile away from where St. Patrick was, the son of King Alphinus (the king of Athcliath) died from sickness. The whole city was in grieving for young Cochadh. Unbelievably, that same day, the King's daughter Dublinia was swimming in a river and drowned. The funeral rites for Cochadh were neglected as droves of people went to the river banks, dove in, and tried to find the body of the princess. Unfortunately, the divers found her at the bottom of the river. They took her body back home and laid her next to her dead brother. The king had lost both of his children in the same day. The grief he must have felt must have been overwhelming.

While they prepared the pagan traditions of burial for the two children, a rumor started going around in the palace that Patrick of Ardmachia, who in the name of an unknown God had raised the dead before, was near the city. King Alphinus asked for Patrick to come, and Patrick did. The king showed Patrick his two dead children and told him that if he raised them from the dead, he and all of his people would worship the God that Patrick served.

Patrick began praying for Dublinia and Cochadh, and before their very eyes, the king and mourners watched as the two children were raised. It was undeniable and incredible. As a result, the king and all of his people abandoned their worship of idols and instead began worshipping the King of Kings. The king and his people were taken to the fountain that Patrick had caused to spring up, and were baptized in it. Then, as a way to remember what God had done that day, the king renamed the city after his daughter that Patrick had raised. Can you guess the name of the city? Dublin.

It gets even better. Since that era and up until relatively recently, on March 17th the Irish would go to the fountain of Patrick and drink their fill of the water that was spurting up from the earth. They would remember what God had done, thank Him for the living water that we have in Christ, and recount the resurrections that Patrick had worked near there. In the last hundred years, this tradition was abandoned (likely due to such gatherings being seen as anti-British activity to the Brits during their occupation of Ireland) and the fountain is now hard to find. It is not unlikely that one reason people copiously drink alcohol on St. Patrick's day nowadays actually stems from this tradition of drinking one's fill of water from The Fountain of Patrick. Incredible.

Time to take it up a notch. Here is a quote from a letter that Patrick sent to a friend,

"The Lord has given to me the power of working miracles...such as are not recorded to have been worked by the Great Apostles...I have raised from the dead bodies that have been buried many years; but I beseech you, let no one believe that for these or the like works I am to be at all equaled with the Apostles...since I am worthy only to be despised."

12th century monk named Jocelyn also wrote this of Patrick,

"For the blind and the lame, the deaf and the dumb, the palsied, the lunatic, the leprous, the epileptic, all who labored under any disease, did he in the Name of the Holy Trinity restore unto the power of their limbs and unto entire health; and in these good deeds was he daily practiced. Thirty and three dead men, some of whom had been many years buried, did this great reviver raise from the dead..."

Did you catch that? Not only did Jocelyn mention thirty-three resurrections that he were aware of in the life of Patrick, but both Patrick and Jocelyn mention that some of the people that Patrick prayed for had been buried "for many years" prior to him raising them up. What follows are testimonies that reflect this reality, but first it would be wise to look at the scriptures for some justification for such miracles. The following testimonies are fantastic…and completely beyond comprehension or any reminiscence of normalcy, even for miracles! In fact, what follows is so wonderfully impossible that maybe that is the reason we have stopped shouting these glorious acts of God from the rooftop. Maybe the following stories are just too much for people, because the world has largely forgotten what God did through Patrick. It is time for that to change! First though, lets refresh our bearing on the truth of the scriptures so that we can fully assimilate the following testimonies into our heart, mind, and spirit so as to not miss out on allowing these stories to become "a spirit of prophecy" in our own lives. Lets make what we are about to talk about scripturally legal.

In John 14:12 Jesus said, "…anyone that has faith in me will do what I have been doing. He will do even greater things than these…"

Don't miss what Christ revealed! Jesus tells us that if we have faith in Him, we can not only do the things that He had been doing, which included raising a decomposing Lazarus out of his tomb, but that we will do greater things than even that. Suddenly, the limiters are taken away. The box is shattered. The gates drop and you are off. This verse is Christ telling you that there is no stopping where you can go with Him or what you can do with Him.

So, what exactly are the "greater things"? The "greater things" is anything that is increasingly impossible to change through natural means. For example, if Lazarus was dead for four days and Christ raised him up, a "greater thing" would be raising the dead after a person has been dead for longer for four days. Patrick tapped into this revelation and didn't hesitate to let Jesus back up His words. Patrick's ability to work uncommon miracles came from the fact that he got ahold of what the scriptures say and actually began to believe it. He must have been in a consistent way of thinking that saw impossible situations as possible. He must have loved to dwell in a place of faith and risk. He saw everything and anything as possible, as nothing would drive a man to pray for the things he did unless this was true.

The next verse that is key when looking at Patrick's life is in Matthew 27. In this chapter, Christ is on the cross and the moment He gives up His spirit the veil is torn. Verses 52 and 53 then go on to say,

"The earth shook and the rocks split. The tombs broke open and the bodies of many holy people who had died were raised to life. They came out of the tombs, and after Jesus' resurrection they went into the holy city and appeared to many people."

If you can, take a minute and let that sink in: Many people that had been literally physically dead literally came out of their tombs, completely restored, walked about, and talked to people. They weren't just raised, but healed, whole, in their right mind, and in love with God. Their bodies, organs, and parts were recreated. They had needed new skin, blood, hair, and a host of other physical body parts. It was a creative miracle as well as resurrection. This is amazing, and a piece of scripture that we regularly overlook or at least do not camp out on enough.

This isn't fable. It isn't myth. It is fact. It happened. This is in THE BIBLE. It is in very translation. It is present in every manuscript that includes the book of

Matthew. And while this portion of scripture is so wild that some biblical scholars try to discredit the fact that it happened simply because it is so incredible, Matthew 27:52-53 stays right there on the pages of our Bibles, staring us in the face and challenging our ability to believe what we profess that we believe: That nothing is impossible with God!

We don't know how long each of the people that were raised had been dead for, but we do know that "many" of them were raised. Some sources say that the number of people that came forth from the graves that day was not in the hundreds, but 10,000. Imagine 10,000 people getting raised from the dead at one time, some dead for quite some time. This is one of the most miraculous events recorded in the Bible, and one of the most overlooked.

It is significant that throughout scripture the word "many" (whether in Hebrew or Greek) wasn't applied to a number less than ten. Instead, the word "many" usually applied to a number ranging from the hundreds to thousands or more. Yet, for the sake of those with a bent like doubting Thomas, lets entertain the most conservative number for what could define "many": let's say six. It is highly unlikely that the verse is referring to only six, as even the "many" at the end of this verse could not be limited to such a small number, but if we were only working with six people that were raised, the point that is needed to be made can still be made. If the number was more, the point is made exponentially.

Ok, here it is. If six people were raised that bittersweet day, the odds that each one had been buried in the previous week is highly unlikely. Less than unlikely actually. Likewise, if there were more than six people that were raised that day, which is more feasible anyways, the odds decrease even more that they had been buried recently. What is much more likely is that those that were raised had been dead for months, years, even decades.

This point is important for many reasons, but one is because it is likely that Patrick saw this verse, did the math, then connected the dots between this verse and John 14:12. Patrick realized that Christ told us that we would do greater things than "these". What are "these?" The miracles that came forth from Jesus' life. Included in that list of miracles is what took place in Matthew 27. It is not unlikely that Patrick saw this wondrous occasion in the Bible and grabbed it for his own, no longer limiting what God was able to do through him, no longer asking questions that elude to excuses, no longer overthinking things. He saw the open arms of the Father in the scriptures and leapt.

Imagine having a loved one that passed 40 years prior suddenly show up at your doorstep, completely healthy and alive. It would be absolutely incredible. Put yourself in the shoes of the people of that day. This actually happened to people.

This has to be said as well: Don't let the imitation and counterfeit that Hollywood sells dilute the gems in scripture; when Jesus does a miracle, people don't come out half-human and distorted. Fear is the best the world can come up with because they don't have the faith that comes from being unconditionally loved. Rest assured that what happened in Matthew 27 wasn't a situation that was scary, weird, or even odd to those that beheld it. Those rudimentary emotions were overridden by the greater realities of beauty and joy that the onlookers experienced when they were reunited with their long lost loved ones. When the Church discovers the power of beauty and compassion that resides in resurrection, the inheritance of power that we have longed for will naturally present itself, but until then we will remain in a foreign land of fear, influenced more by graphic, fictional movies rather than what the Bible clearly declares.

When looking at this portion of scripture we get insight into the fact that families were restored that day after years of being fractured and broken. Mothers and fathers received back their sons and daughters. Sons and daughters received back parents. Grief was stopped in its tracks, tears dried up, long unexpected embraces took the place of the song of the dirge. Joy replaced sadness. Simply said, death had been overcome by this carpenter from Nazareth. It was beautiful. Talk about a ministry of reconciliation!

Now for the testimonies. Once Patrick entered an area called Fearta with a crowd of people following from him. He learned of two women that had died and were buried on a hill nearby, and made his way there. The story seems to imply that the women hadn't been buried recently. Upon arrival he "commanded the earth to be removed", then prayed for the two women to be raised to life. They were, in full view of the bystanders. It isn't clear if he commanded someone nearby to uncover the bodies, or if he actually commanded the earth to open and give up the bodies therein. Either way, the women were brought to life and all that beheld this miracle were brought into the Kingdom that day.

Another time Patrick was in a place called Humestia. The prince of Humestia was won over by Patrick's preaching then baptized, but had a hard time believing that a body that had deteriorated to the point of dust could be resurrected at the end of time back to the pristine state. Patrick showed him what the scriptures say about the resurrection, but the prince still wasn't convinced. The prince said, "If in the name of Jesus you raise my grandfather that has been dead many days, I'll believe what you say about the resurrection." Patrick went to the tomb of the grandfather, had the tomb opened, then made a sign of the cross with his staff. The grandfather got up, raised from the dead after many days. The grandfather began telling people of his experience in hell and his desire to be baptized. It goes without saying that the prince relented in his lack of faith on the issue of resurrection.

Many times when people are raised from the dead they speak of the place they were experiencing moments prior; hell. Rather than taking shots trying to figure out how exactly hell works, let us not miss the overarching revelation that Patrick's life demonstrates to us: People can be seemingly pulled out of an justified, eternal situation of torment because of another person's obedience to Christ's command in Matthew 10:8 to "raise the dead". This is nothing short of phenomenal.

Take that in for a moment. It flips everything we have ever known pertaining to heaven and hell on its head. We know that without Christ we find ourselves in hell. That much is clear. Thus, it is nothing less than absolute surprise, nothing less than undiluted grace, that another imperfect human has the capability, through the power of the Holy Spirit, to pull another person out of an eternal situation of horror that they put themselves into. It must simply mean that God's love and power are greater than hell (Matt. 16:18), that Christ overcame hell and the grave (Rev. 1:18), and that if we will have faith, the magnitude of even our small acts of courage have the potential to shake not only this world, but the ones to come after this life is over.

Once Patrick and some disciples were walking and passed by an enormous tomb. They stopped, looking at its incredible length, wondering how tall the person sealed in it must have been. More than a leading of the Spirit, it seems that Patrick and his comrades were simply curious how tall the guy was. This prompted them to pray for him to be raised. A massive man opened the tomb and came out. He was so tall that he is described as a giant, and that his height was nothing less than "terrifying". Let's assume he was at least nine feet tall, though the account reads in a way that gives the feeling that he may have been even taller. When the man saw Patrick, he started weeping, thanking him for praying him back to life as he had been in hell and anyone that could spare him from even a moment of what he had been experiencing he would be indebted to forever. He asked Patrick if he could go with him and his men to wherever they were headed. Patrick told him no because he was too tall and would bring them too much unneeded attention. That is hilarious considering it was coming from the guy who went around raising people from the dead...like they didn't have a lot attention already. The tall man relented in his desire, and Patrick asked him his name. The man told them that his name was Glarcus, the son of a man named Chaiis, that he was one hundred years old when he died, and that he been killed in an ambush by a man named Fynnan Mac Con. Patrick told him to believe in the Father, Son, and the Holy Spirit, and the man did. Not long after that the man died again, now headed to heaven rather than the place of torment he had been so graciously freed from.

Patrick began to have such a significant impact for the gospel in Ireland that pagans who were opposed to the message of Christ got concerned. They were worried that if more regions were won to the gospel by Patrick, the laws that enabled them to do shameful religious pagan rituals would be taken away. Thus, they went and found a woman who was washing flax in an area that Patrick was going to be passing through. In an attempt to frame him, they forced the woman to hide the majority of her flax in a nearby tree and to blame Patrick of theft when he walked by. The woman did as instructed her, and the pagans jumped out from their hiding place and grabbed Patrick, shouting that the only fitting sentence for such a theft was death.

Nearby was a tomb. While under citizen arrest, Patrick prayed for the man to be raised that was inside, as he didn't have any witness to the truth of his situation beside this dead man. The man came out from the tomb protesting Patrick's innocence, then went over to the tree and showed the gathering crowd the hidden flax and the truth of the matter. Thus, Patrick was released, forgave the people that had tried to frame and kill him, then led anyone that wanted salvation to Jesus. There are so many stories like this in the life of Patrick that they all cannot be covered here. There is a story that Patrick grew tiresome of the snakes in Ireland so he simply commanded them to leave...the entire country. It is said that the snakes left in droves. There was Ethra, the wife of a man named Euchadius. Ethra died and was carried by her husband to Patrick, promising to give himself to Jesus if he worked this miracle for him. Patrick did and chalked a few more up to the Kingdom.

It must be said that though there is wonderful fruit

as the result of someone being raised in these stories, the sole reason God raises the dead is not just so that someone gives their life to Jesus. God raises the dead because He is life. The dead are raised not as a means to an end but because it is the manifestation of the nature of God. A resurrection miracle is still beautiful even if someone doesn't give their life to Jesus afterwards because it is a sign and wonder that nonetheless points to the goodness of God. We owe the world an encounter with God regardless if they want to be thankful to God for it or not. When we get in a mindset that only values a miracle if it results in someone getting saved we miss the beauty of Who the miracle points to rather than what it accomplished.

And now for the grand finale from the life of Patrick of Ardmachia. In a 900-year-old historical document, it says that once Patrick was preaching to a group of people about the reality of hell. Patrick, like Paul, wasn't satisfied with only talking about the Kingdom but believed that the message must also be demonstrated. Thus, Patrick went to the graves of nineteen men, bringing the people he had been preaching to with him. In front of everyone he raised each and every person that was dead and buried, one by the name of Fotus that had been dead for ten years. One by one, each person that was raised then began testifying to the listeners of the reality of hell and exhorted the people to listen to what Patrick was saying as they had been experiencing hell just moments before, prior to them being raised. They assured the people that hell was not a place anyone would want to go, and needless to say, the people listened and gave their hearts to the Lord.

Inevitably, Patrick's life will be written off as myth

by some but for those with the faith of a child his life increases wonder and worship for God. In fact, Patrick knew that the signs and wonders that sprung from his life would sound unbelievable to people. In anticipation of that, he said this of the signs and wonders that followed him:

"Let those that will laugh and scorn do so. I shall not be silent nor will I hide the signs and wonders which the Lord has shown me."

Patrick worked miracles because of His constant connection to the Father. He did as he saw the Father doing. Let's believe for the "greater things you will do", stay connected to Papa, and as a result, change whole nations, just as Patrick did.

Zenobius of Florence
(337AD-417AD)

Zenobius (sometimes referred to as Zanobi) was raised in an unbelieving family but was quickly drawn to the gospel at a relatively young age. Once he gave his life to prayer, signs and wonders followed him regularly. There were five people that Zenobius raised from the dead.

The first occurrence took place when a mother left her sick child with Zenobius in hopes that when she returned he would be healthy. Unfortunately, the opposite happened; the child got more sick and when the mother returned, he died. The mother, knowing Zenobius' faith, asked him to pray and bring him back from death. Zenobius did as the mother asked, prayed, then made a sign of the cross over the boy. The boy returned to life and Zenobius handed the child back to the mother, totally restored.

Zenobius' second manifest victory over the spirit of death took place primarily because of the above story. A mother and father who had lost their son and on their way to bury him in the graveyard had heard of the miracle that God did for the mother of the sick boy and basically demanded that Zenobius do the same for them. Zenobius obliged, touched the body of the young man, and lifted his eyes to heaven in prayer. Immediately, the boy's spirit returned to his body.

There is something about breakthrough that has a domino effect in our lives. Once something is yours in the Kingdom, it will continue to be yours and will be added to as you steward what God has done. For Zenobius, his first breakthrough into resurrection resulted in more taking place, like this story of his third raising.

Another monk named Simplicius, a contemporary of Zenobius, was riding a horse one day when something went terribly wrong and he was thrown off a tall cliff. Not only did the fall kill him, but his body was badly mangled. Zenobius prayed and Simplicius was brought back to life. In 1433, John Tortel wrote the following statement describing the result Zenobius' prayers: "… rehabilitated the body so entirely that no vestige of the accident was discernable".

How awesome would it be for the Church to once again become a group of people so known for their ability to so completely rehabilitate a body from sickness or death that no vestige of what afflicted them was discernable! What if we became so good at allowing God to heal through us and raise the dead that unbelievers came to followers of Christ before going to the doctor! This, and more, is available to us.

Forth, while Zenobius and two of his friends were at a church a child was run over by a carriage. The infant had been playing in front of the church and after being ran over, was inspected and found to be deceased. Zenobius, Eugenius, and Crescentius (those are some epic names by the way) were nearby and began praying over the child. Akin to the last story, after prayer the once-victim was not only raised but was restored to such a degree that it was as though the accident never happened.

Every vein and stream of the Church has its problems, including both Catholicism and Protestantism. But overshadowing the errors and mistakes people make within these structures of belief are stories of compassion and care like three grown men running to a little child that has just been ran over by a carriage, pouring their heart out to God, and God restoring the child's life. When we hear these kinds of testimonies, faith in the Church, and in humanity in general, is restored. Regardless of what has happened to you in the Church, let these stories convince you that there are people out there that want nothing less than "peace on earth, and good will to men." There really are servants of God, out to give rather than take.

Zanobius' fifth and last rezzy took place with Eugenius, from the above story. Eugenius' father had died and Eugenius felt led to bring him back to life, so he went to Zanobius and asked him what to do. Zanobius told him to sprinkle him with some water and believe. Eugene did this and his father was instantly raised and in good health.

Benedict of Nursia
(480AD-547AD)

Benedict's life is one of a kind not only because he raised the dead but because the testimonies and facets of his life where recounted by the Pope himself. Most of the information on Benedict that we have today is because of Pope Gregory (540ad-604ad), and it is wisdom to remember that in those days the knowledge of resurrections taking place was not something limited to a minority fringe group but instead, belonged to the whole of the Church, including the top tier leadership including and especially, the Pope.

Benedict is recorded to have raised two people. The first was a desperate father whose son had died. When the father told Benedict to raise his son, Benedict told the father no. His reasoning wasn't because he didn't want to, but because he had never raised the dead before and thought that it was something only the "holy apostles" could do. Nonetheless, the father kept pleading with Benedict, then upped the ante by saying that he wouldn't leave Benedict's side until he prayed for his son. There probably isn't better motivation for a monk (a person dedicated to alone time and prayer) than to be told that they would not be left alone until they relent. And relent Benedict did, suddenly asking where the body of the young man was. The father led Benedict to the gate of the monastery, and Benedict bent down to pray over him. After he prayed it is said that the young man's body began to twitch and shake. The witnesses concluded that God was doing something, so Benedict bent down once again and scooped up the boy in his arms. When he handed the boy over to his dad the shaking stopped and a healthy, joyful, young man was looking back at his father. Beautiful.

We will all find ourselves in spots while on this earth where the demands put on us seem impossible. They are. But that is when a person must lean into God and throw themselves into the situation with full force. If you have never raised the dead, when someone dies it is time to remember that the same Spirit that raised Christ from the dead lives in you. Experience is priceless, but prior to experience becoming a reality you already possess something of even greater value: God Himself. Don't hesitate or question yourself if you are put in an impossible situation. God has your back. Move in confidence.

Benedict's second resurrection took place in the midst of the monk's working on one of the monastery walls. Supposedly, the enemy actually came and mocked Benedict while he was alone in his prayer room, saying that he was about to go "visit" one of the monks. Immediately, Benedict sent word to the monks to be on high-alert because the enemy was on his way to harm them. The message didn't get there in time and the wall came crashing down unexpectedly, completely decimating a young monk, crushing his body. The young man's body was so damaged that they were not able to simply pick it up. Instead, they slid a blanket under the remains, grasp the four corners of the cloth, and carried him to Benedict's prayer room. Benedict had the destroyed body laid on his prayer mat, then told everyone to leave the room. An hour later the young man suddenly joined his fellow monks at the wall and to their astonishment, even began to work alongside them on the wall. He was raised and healthy with no broken bones, scratches, or even a bruise! Talk about a backfire for the enemy.

·

Columba of Iona
(521AD-597AD)

Columba was another Celtic hero of old. He raised the dead, worked incredible miracles, and brought the Gospel in power everywhere he traveled.

One example of resurrection took place when Columba was in the province of the Picts. A countryman had heard the Gospel and had given himself to It. A few days later his son became extremely sick. The druid Magi, instead of consoling the family, began verbally abusing the father because of his decision to give his life to God, arguing that the sickness was due to his decision to follow Jesus rather than the gods of old. Columba was informed of the situation and came to the home of the father. When he arrived, the child had already succumbed to death. Columba first comforted the family, then asked if he could be led to where the child's body was. The father took him to the child, and Columba knelt down next to the body, his face streaming with tears. Then standing back up, he stared at the boy and said, "In the name of Jesus, arise and stand upon your feet." The boy opened his eyes, Columba outstretched his hand, and the boy took it, standing to his feet. Columba then led the boy out of the room and back to his family. The shouting of the people became undignified and loud, tears had been turned to joy, and God was glorified.

When we remember that death is an enemy (1 Cor. 15:26), it keeps us from insulating ourselves from feeling the loss that death brings. When we fail to remember that death is an enemy, we view death as a comrade of sorts and we are unable to have empathy, compassion, or any sense of conviction when death steals a loved one from someone. Any time we are unable to access compassion for someone in the midst of their loss, we have likely adopted a paradigm that is unlike God's. The ability to be broken on other's behalf is not only a gift from God, but part of His very nature. Let us adopt a view on life and death that allows us to weep with those that weep and embody the Answer for those with looming question borne from loss.

Chapter Two
(550AD-1200AD)

"What we love we shall grow to resemble."
-Bernard of Clairvaux

Winefride of Holywell
(600AD-650AD)

The account of Winefride differs from the other stories in this book in that Winefride wasn't the one to raise the dead, but the one that was raised. Nonetheless, it is a marvelous story of resurrection.

Growing up, Winefride was influenced by the teachings of a monk named Beuno, resulting in her decision to take vows of celibacy, a love offering to Christ.

One day a young man named Caradoc, the son of the King of Northern Wales, came to visit Winefride to ask for her hand in marriage. Winefride's father was a wealthy noble and it was thought that the two of them would be a good match. Shortly into their time together, Winefride quickly discerned Caradoc's intentions were based around motives of lust rather than more wholesome intentions, and moreso that her safety was at stake because Caradoc could obviously not control his desires. She quickly devised a plan and told Caradoc that she needed to go to her room to change into a more beautiful dress for him. He bought it. Instead of returning, Winefride fled towards the church where her parents were listening to Beuno preach. Somehow though, Caradoc caught on, chased her down with a sword, and intercepted her before she could make it inside the church building.

As he stared at her intimidatingly he said, "Once I loved you and desired to hold you in my embrace. You have fled from me when I came to you; you have rejected me. Yield to me now or else this sword shall put an end to your life, for I will cut off your head."

Winefride boldly turned to Caradoc and said, "I am betrothed to the Son of the Eternal King, the Judge of all mankind. No other spouse can I receive; no other will I have while I live. Draw your sword, and exert all your strength and ferocity; but be sure that neither terror nor flattery, promises or threats, will ever draw me away from the sweetness of His love, to whom my own love and devotion are pledged." On the spot, Caradoc drew his sword and cut off Winefride's head.

The people soon discovered what had happened and were horrified. Beuno gathered people in the church and everyone there began to pray for Winefride's life to be restored. Beuno physically set Winefride's head back on the body and after some time of prayer it miraculously attached, she began to breathe, and life was restored to her.

A fountain spring sprang up from the spot where Winefride's head fell to the ground and to this day can be visited in Holywell, United Kingdom. It seems that the Presence of God still resides in that place, as a father once brought his deceased baby daughter to the well and left the body there overnight. The body was wrapped and prepared for burial. When he came back the next morning, he found his daughter crawling about on the ground, restored and unbound. The child was weak and immediately asked for food but other than that, completely healthy.

As a sidenote, minutes after Winefride was brought to life after being murdered it is said that Caradoc suddenly died. The best way to keep death off your doorstep is by exuding life. The quickest way to let the enemy into your life to steal, kill, and destroy (John

10:10) is by stealing, killing, and destroying. The same way you live many times dictates the nature of your death. Live by the sword, die by the sword.

Stanislaus of Cracow
(1030AD-1079AD)

Stanislaus lived out his life and ministry in Cracow, under the reign of the brutal king Boleslaw II and to this day is regarded to be one of the greater commanders of the faith in Poland.

Boleslaw was a continual "thorn in the flesh" to Stanislaus throughout his entire time in ministry, one of the most prominent conflicts being over who owned the property that Stanislaus' church was built on. Boleslaw claimed it was his (as though he didn't already have enough land as king), and Stanislaus said it was his own.

King Boleslaw never liked Stanislaus, likely because Stanislaus lived a righteous life that threatened Boleslaw. Righteousness has a way of offending people if they don't yet understand grace. It is more than possible that Stanislaus' life naturally convicted Boleslaw, and the king never learned how to handle that very well.

The testimony goes like this. A man named Peter Miles sold property to Stanislaus that later became the place where the church was built. Not long after that, Peter passed. Three years after Peter Miles died, Boleslaw went to Peter's sons and conspired with them to make claims against Stanislaus that he had possessed the property through fraud. The information brought against Stanislaus seemed more substantial than the proof that Stanislaus could produce, thus the judge would rule in favor of Boleslaw and Stanislaus would lose the property and the church. In reality, Boleslaw simply didn't want Stanislaus in ministry anymore, and was willing to lie in an attempt to remove him.

Stanislaus asked the judge for a three-day delay in the hearing, after which he said he would produce the dead man himself as a witness. Yes, you read that correctly. The only person that had enough credibility to change the direction of the court case was Peter Mills, thus Stanislaus publicly made the claim that he would bring Peter back from the dead after three years so that he could testify on Stanislaus' behalf. The judge granted Stanislaus the three days. Along with the granted request came ridicule, laugher, and mockery coming from both Stanislaus' enemies and acquaintances.

One cannot survive traversing the persecution, heartache, and pressure like what Stanislaus went through unless they are caught up in God's love to such an extent that blissful ignorance and obliviousness takes precedence over condemnation. When seated with Christ in heavenly places, nothing dark that happens or is said on earth can affect a person. They are invulnerable.

Stanislaus prayed and fasted for three days. On the third day, not long before the court reconvened, Stanislaus led a procession of people that had attended Mass to the graveside of Peter Miles. Stanislaus prayed over the grave, then had it opened. Lying before them was nothing but the bones of Peter Miles, who had been dead for three years.

Stanislaus then touched the bones of Miles and ordered the dead man to rise. Before an awed crowd of both believers and unbelievers the bones suddenly came together and were covered by flesh, and Peter Miles came to life. Peter grabbed Stanislaus' outstretched hand and was led to the trial.

Boleslaw was waiting in the courtroom with his false witnesses, excited to publicly dishonor and embarrass Stanislaus, then take his land. To his and everyone else's surprise, Peter Mills walked into the courtroom as Stanislaus in biblical proportions declared, "Behold Peter! He has come to give his testimony. Interrogate him. He will answer you!"

They interrogated Peter the best they could considering their stupor and amazement, and in the end, Stanislaus was obviously acquitted. Boleslaw did not repent that day despite Stanislaus exhortation to do so, though he likely did years later, but only after his hatred led him to martyr Stanislaus with his own hands. Sometimes it takes blood to fertilize the ground that the seed is thrown into before it sprouts and takes root.

Bernard of Abbeville
(1046AD-1117AD)

Bernard of Abbeville was the founder of an abbey and a order of monks, but more importantly, believed Christ actually meant it when He told the Church to raise the dead. Bernard started as a monk and stayed at the monastery until he was disapproved to become the new abbot by his superiors. After that, he promptly became a hermit. Many forerunners are not given the place they should be given because their message is not widely understood at first. The message of a forerunner is not meant to impress but actually make a difference in the world, thus the outcome is that many times they are cast out from normal church life. Unfortunately, they simply do not fit in. Bernard became a hermit but did not abandon his love for God nor did he allow bitterness towards the Church to overtake his heart. These are the two challenges for every forerunner, and if they can navigate these two issues correctly, they will always succeed in making known the message that was given to them. As a hermit, over time Bernard slowly attracted others to him. He led them, not unlike David and his mighty men, raising up giant slayers in hidden places. The following account was given by Geoffroy le Gros, one of Bernard's disciples.

Bernard was summoned to a harvesting field where a nun had been run over by a heavy cart, pulled by ten bulls. Her body was mangled and unsightly, but Bernard laid his hands on her and commanded her to be healed and restored to life. At his word she did, not showing any trace of the accident.

In every setting where the enemy has stolen, killed, or destroyed it is easy to look at what is impossible in the situation. Everyone has unconscious boundaries on faith that are only revealed and discovered when they face impossible situations. We (the DRT) have heard every reason why the dead shouldn't be able to be raised: embalming fluid, missing limbs, decapitation, irrevocably burned, dead "too long", death by suicide, an unbeliever that is in hell, cremation, the family members aren't believers, on and on. The sky is the limit when dealing with unbelief. The reasons why someone cannot be raised from the dead are as numerous as we want them to be, but greater is the Reason they can be raised; Christ.

Christ is greater. Regardless of the situation, remind yourself that nothing is impossible with God. The body was mangled and crushed by a cart then tramped by ten bulls; Nothing is impossible with God. The body has been embalmed; Nothing is impossible with God. They have been dead for years; Nothing is impossible with God. The person was decapitated; Nothing is impossible with God. The body has been burned; Nothing is impossible with God. The body has been cremated; Nothing is impossible with God. The person committed suicide; Nothing is impossible with God. The person is in hell; Nothing is impossible with God. The person is in heaven; Nothing is impossible with God.

Having been put into many of these resurrection situations, this has become the mantra that I repeat and must allow to continually affect my spirit and mind. I have to remind myself of this truth, but I also have to remind others. And honestly, some people let it apprehend their understanding and renew their mind, and some just go along with it because it is in scripture and they have to. They look at me with an expression that says, "Well yeah, I can't argue with you because it is the Bible, but really man, let's be realistic."

It isn't that I don't see the impossibilities in front of me or that I am ignoring them. It is that I am choosing, despite the mountain in front of me, to believe that the problem can be tossed into the sea though its size is insurmountable.

God can. You can't. And that is the real issue; the only time confusion and unbelief raise their heads are when we think everything is about us. In the end it is our narcissism that cuts us short. If we realize it isn't about us but everything is about Him, impossibilities vanish. Boundaries on faith dissolve and the wonder of green fields of possibility open us before us where we are welcomed to dance with joy and expectation.

Bernard of Clairvaux
(1090AD-1153AD)

Bernard of Clairvaux has been long considered by Catholics to be one of the greatest miracle workers ever to have walked the earth. It is likely that the vast amount of healings, dead raisings, and divine interventions that took place in Bernard's life were not recorded, but of the ones that were written down, even secular historians that were harsh and critical towards the validation of supernatural events had to relent and admit that the overwhelming proof pointed to the fact that these claimed events did actually occur. The following story of resurrection is an example.

Bernard was preaching near Constance, traveling about with a knight that he had won to the Lord. The knight had a squire that was unhappy about the knight's conversion and would regularly shout threats and insults at them when they were ministering to people. Once while they were about to pray for a crippled lady, they saw the squire approaching, enraged at their audacity to pray for someone so sick. In full view of the squire, they prayed for the woman and she was healed. The moment the squire saw the woman stand up, no longer crippled, he fell down dead. Maybe it was shock, maybe it was something unseen was finally given entrance to steal, kill, and destroy. Whatever it was, it took the squire's life.

Knowing that the miracle was the straw that broke the camel's back, Bernard felt somewhat responsible for what had happened, was heart broke and exclaimed, "God forbid that someone should die on my account!" He went to the body, told the people around him to hold the man's head, then prayed the Our Father prayer and anointed the squire's head with his spit. The squire regained life and stood up. Bernard then forcefully asked him, "What is your disposition? What do you want to do now?"

The squire gave his life to the Lord on the spot, relayed to Bernard and the people nearby that he had just been in a court where he had just been found guilty and was going to be taken away to hell. He told the people that if Bernard had not intervened, he would presently be in hell. Literally. The squire and the knight both went on to serve the Lord the rest of their days.

This puts quite a different spin on resurrection, doesn't it? Do we realize that resurrection is not just a sign and a wonder that glorifies God but a tool of salvation? Resurrection is the saving arm of the Lord, long enough and strong enough to reach into deep places of pit and mire and pull His children back into light and love. If we do not use this wonderful tool God has given us, those that could be spared from potential horror, simply, will not be.

Be a hero. Pray to raise the dead.

Dominic of Osma
(1170AD-1221AD)

Dominic was one of those men that loved God and not only did not seek the spotlight, but did everything he could to stay out of it. Those that possess true authority and power aren't like that because of a false humility but because if word gets out of the legitimate power that they have, the undesired attention would cause them to lose the very things that got them to the place they are at: the ability to spend long times alone with God. Some people genuinely enjoy changing the world from behind the scenes rather than being the guy holding a microphone.

Dominic was indirectly influenced by Benedict of Nursia (Chapter One), and gave his life to prayer at the young age of twenty-five. By the end of his life Dominic had established the Dominican order, which is still present on the earth today. The following stories communicate what would cause this man to be emulated by so many people.

Once Dominic was in Rome building his first convent. A lady named Guatenia came to hear Dominic's preaching. In doing so, she left her sick son at home. Unfortunately, when she returned back to her house she found her son had died while she was away. She wept in grief for a long time, overwhelmed by her loss. Suddenly the thought of God's love crashed in on her, and it gave her the hope to pray for her son's life to be restored. She reasoned that since God is merciful and Dominic was nearby a miracle could happen. Her son's body was carried by servants and she set out for the convent.

When she found Dominic, she knelt down at his feet

and laid the boy's body at his feet. She said nothing but simply cried at his feet. Dominic excused himself for a moment to pray. He returned, made the sign of the cross over the boy, then grabbed the boy's hand and raised him to his feet. The boy was not only resurrected, but the sickness that had taken his life was instantly healed as well.

A few friars nearby witnessed the miracle and went to the pope to tell him about it. The pope turned around and had the miracle made know to the public in Rome, despite Dominic's request against it. Dominic's concerns were validated when he was mobbed by fans in the street. The people of Rome so revered him that they literally ripped some of his clothes off as he walked through the city, in hopes that in touching just the garments that he had worn, miracles would invade their life. Sounds like something Jesus dealt with as well.

Once during the construction of the same convent in Rome (San Sisto Vecchio), an architect was in the cellars when a landslide sealed him in. By the time they had dug him out, he was dead. The monks got extremely fearful that the public would see such an incident as God's displeasure upon the convent, and Dominic noticed their concerns. Dominic had the body brought to him, prayed, and raised him on the spot.

Another time a body of a young man was brought to Dominic who had fallen off a horse and been trampled, leaving his body without life and quite mangled. Dominic had the body brought to a room and locked it inside. He then went and led mass, where witnesses claimed that not unlike Christ in His ascension back to heaven, Dominic rose off the ground while in communion with God. After returning to the ground, Dominic made his way to the room, prayed for the mangled body, and in calling the man's spirit back to his body, raised him to life. His body was no longer mangled, and early biographers recorded this miracle as a resurrection miracle. Through these miracles the Dominican order was established, now all over the earth. There are many other miracles, even resurrections, that took place in Dominic's life (like the time he stretched out on a man like Elijah, and restored him), but to cover them all here would be too timely.

Dominic is a great example to us of a man that walked in such genuine power that the world took notice. He had no need to promote himself or seek influence because he had real power. Real power that is led and submitted to Holy Spirit always seeks to stay out of the spotlight as they already have more promotion and influence than any man can steward very well. It is wisdom to stay off the radar of humanity.

Chapter Three
(1185AD-1300AD)

.

"The creator of the heavens obeys a carpenter;
the God of eternal glory listens to a poor virgin.
Has anyone ever witnessed anything comparable to this?
Let the philosopher no longer disdain from listening to
the common laborer;
the wise, to the simple;
the educated, to the illiterate;
a child of a prince, to a peasant."
-St. Anthony of Padua

Hyacinth of Poland
(1185AD-1257AD)

Hyacinth was born in Poland and his studies took him around the world. While he was in Rome he witnessed Dominic (Chapter Two) work a miracle firsthand. After seeing God work so clearly through Dominic, Hyacinth abandoned the direction his life was headed in and became a friar. You never know what working one miracle is going to do; Hyacinth not only went on to influence many for the Gospel, but it is said that he likely raised around fifty people from the dead. What follows are a few of those accounts.

Hyacinth is unique because many of his resurrection miracles had to do with those that died from drowning. The first time he raised someone back from death by drowning he was at the Vistula River, about to cross. A woman suddenly approached him, carrying the body of a boy. The woman turned out to be a widow and the boy she was carrying was her only son, Peter. While Peter had drowned the night before, the body had been recovered only a few minutes prior to her approaching Hyacinth.

Hyacinth began to cry on the widow's behalf. He was moved by her loss, her faith, and her love. He then grabbed the boy's hand and prayed, "Peter, may our Lord Jesus Christ, whose glory I preach, restore you to life!"

It did not take long. Peter stood to his feet, thanking God and Hyacinth immediately.

The next resurrection Hyacinth prayed for was alike to Peter's in that it involved a young man that had drowned, but also differed in a wonderful way. A woman named Primislava had sent her son (Vislaus) to Hyacinth to request that he come and preach to her and a group of people she had gathered. On the way back home after making the request to Hyacinth, out of haste the young man decided to take an old bridge to cross the Raba river. The bridge gave way and Vislaus drowned. A witness of the accident sent word to Primislava, and she arrived on the scene the time that Hyacinth did, on his way to preach to Primislava's people. The body had not been recovered, and Primislava was extremely distraught. Vislaus was her only child and couldn't even give him a proper burial due to the fact that they didn't have a body.

At this point, many of us may give up. We would reason in the natural and not think supernaturally; we would tell ourselves that we can't pray for the boy as we don't know where he is! The truth is that God knows where the boy's body is, and that when we pray in faith remembering that God is all powerful and all knowing, we do Him justice and honor.

Hyacinth prayed and suddenly the body appeared. One source says that the body suddenly floated to the surface of the river and despite the current, floated to the shore where Hyacinth and the broken mother were standing. Another source says that the body literally appeared. Either way, what is important is they had recovered the body!

Primislava reasoned in her mind, connecting the dots. She said to Hyacinth, "Your prayers have recovered his body; they can restore his life!"

Hyacinth agreed, went over to the body and touched him. He prayed, "Vislaus, my son, may our Lord Jesus Christ, who gives life to all things, resuscitate you." Vislaus got up off the ground, raised to life. By this time there was a crowd near by, and they broke into praise.

Cyril of Constantinople
(1191AD-1235AD)

Cyril of Constantinople is unique in that his miracles are of a different sort. Once he gave a coin to a blind man that was begging. Not long after, the blind man pieced together that it was Cyril that had given him the coin. Thus, in faith, the blind man held the coin up to his eyes. He was instantly healed. Inspired by the miracle, the man that had been blind then went directly to a monastery nearby. Some of the monastery leadership was gone, so they turned the man away. He left brokenhearted and died of an illness a few days later. Cyril heard the news, went and found his body, and raised him back to life.

Cyril is also credited with raising someone after he had already passed himself, not unlike Elijah. The story goes like this. After Cyril had passed away, a young man that was on his way to Israel aboard a boat died. The when the boat was in port, the captain went to the Carmelite monks in the area and asked them to give the young man a fitting burial. The monks agreed, and took the body to a cemetery, the same cemetery where Cyril had been buried. They went to lay the body out on the tomb of Cyril while they dug a grave for the young man, but the moment the body touched the tomb of Cyril, he came to life and exclaimed: "Cyril has restored me to life and reserved me for a better!" Being that the man had been dead, he would have had no knowledge of his body being laid on Cyril's tomb unless Cyril had somehow visited him wherever he was when he was dead. Very interesting and intriguing.

While we have a vague grasp of how things function

on the other side, our understanding of the spirit realm, heaven, and hell is by no means a science. We have no formulation to how resurrection works. We just know it happens. How it takes place is altogether different every time. It is good to keep an open mind about these realities, thereby not creating beliefs or doctrines that the nature and acts of God later shatter anyways. We may as well just stick to "God is love" and let everything else fall into its rightful place.

Anthony of Padua
(1195AD-1231AD)

When it comes to men of God that have pioneered in realms of faith, anointing, and the Kingdom of God, one that shines is Anthony of Padua. In his short life (36 years) he made quite an impact, even influencing his own contemporaries like Francis of Assisi. Anthony's humility, miracles, faith and eloquence were obviously hard to not take notice. He is credited with raising the dead twelve times. Anthony regularly walked in the prophetic on an extremely high level, but he also possessed less common spiritual abilities like speaking to people when he was not geographically near them, being transported, and showing up in multiple locations at once. He would regularly go to cities that were known to have resisted the Gospel and would have success where others had failed, turning the region to God. This happened so many times that he was dubbed "The Hammer of Heretics". Interestingly, San Antonio in Texas is named after Anthony of Padua. In fact, if a person goes inside the Alamo in downtown San Antonio, they will find a statue of Anthony serving as a reminder of the inheritance and calling the state of Texas and the United States has to resurrection, intimacy with Jesus, and reaching the nations for the Kingdom of God. Anthony's influence on the globe cannot be done justice by being written about in one book, let alone just part of a chapter, but nonetheless here are some of the incredible miracles Anthony worked.

There is an account of a young man that was so upset with his mother that he kicked her. Later he went to his mother to ask for forgiveness, but she rejected his proposal. Misled, emotionally unstable, and deceived by religious guilt, the young man used a hatchet to cut off the foot that he had kicked his mother with. Anthony was in the area, heard about what had happened, and went to the young man. After seeing the heart of the misguided youth, he assured him that he had been forgiven by God for what he had done to his mother. Anthony took hold of the man's damaged leg with one hand and with the other he grabbed the severed foot. Anthony joined the leg and the foot together as he prayed and the two parts became one again, working as perfectly as they had before the hatchet had been used. Another time, Anthony was invited to dine with his enemies. He gladly accepted the invitation. The hosts poisoned his food, but little did the hosts know, God had already made Anthony aware of this reality. Anthony prayed out loud, "I eat this food not for the design of tempting God, but of showing my zeal for the salvation of these souls!" He then, by faith, ate. All "enemies" that were present gave their lives to Jesus that night, due to the fact that Anthony did not die.

The most well know story from the life of Anthony has been captured in paintings hung in churches across Europe in addition to being written about in various credible documents. At the time of this story's unfolding, Anthony was serving at a monastery in Padua, which was a 12 days walk from the city that his family lived in, Lisbon, Spain. One day in Lisbon, a man was murdered and Anthony's father was framed for the crime. The trial was scheduled to be held only a few days after the crime took place, and because of the time it would take for someone to travel to Anthony's monastery to deliver the news of the accusation, it would be impossible for Anthony to be present during the hearing. Nonetheless, during prayer God made Anthony aware of the situation, and after gaining permission to leave the monastery, Anthony began the long journey to Lisbon on foot. Even by horseback there was no possible way that Anthony could make it to Lisbon in time to catch the trial, but he went anyways, rationalizing that maybe he could be of some help after the bogus verdict of guilt had been issued to his father.

As soon as Anthony left the outskirts of his city, he found himself walking through the doors of the courthouse and into the room where the trial was taking place in Lisbon. He had been transported from one city to the other. All present knew there was no way Anthony could have known about his father's situation, as well as gotten to the hearing with such speed, thus his arrival alone spoke overtly of God's divine work in the situation. All fell silent as Anthony made his way to the judge in the front of the room.

Anthony declared that his father was innocent, and in reply, the judge asked for proof to such a claim. Full of the boldness that comes upon a person when they are in the anointing for faith, Anthony replied, "The murdered man shall bear witness as to the truth of my testimony." He then led the people, including the judge and jury, to the grave of the man that had been murdered.

When they arrived, Anthony asked that the grave be opened and the body uncovered. He then commanded the dead man to speak to the crowd and tell the people of his father's innocence. Just as Anthony commanded, the dead man sat up and spoke, telling all that were present that Anthony's father was innocent. Astonished, and still in need of bringing punishment upon whoever committed this crime, the judges asked who was guilty, because

Anthony's father was obviously blameless. Anthony replied, "I come to declare the innocent, not to denounce the guilty." Incredible.

Think of the faith, the risk, that it would take to stand before family and friends and declare that you could prove your father's innocence by raising a murdered man from the dead. Even after the hundreds of years since this miracle took place, one can still hear the echoing silence of that room after Anthony declared that the dead man would tell them himself. Faith is sometimes most evident in continuing to believe when everyone in the room has gone deadly quiet.

It is to these types of men and women, those with nothing to lose, lacking all fear of man, with such focus and passion for the face of God, that a spirit resurrection power resides and dwells with. It is to those that leap that are caught, to those that risk that are rewarded, and those that believe that see what is otherwise unseen.

Anthony had his fair share of challenges, but unfavorable circumstances seemed to cause his persistence and tenacity for the Kingdom to come to light even more. One such situation was in Rimini, near the river Marecchia. Anthony had been exhorting the people of that area to give their lives to Jesus. His efforts were met by ridicule and mockery and after some time, nobody seemed to care to listen to him. He confronted the situation by saying, "Since you have shown yourself unworthy to hear the word of God, behold, I turn to the fishes, that your unbelief may be put to shame." So, he turned to the river and began to preach to the fish in the water. He began reminding the fish of all the benefits of God creating them; of clear water, of the freedom He gave them, and how He fed them without any labor on their part. It sounds insane, but the scriptures clearly say in Mark 16:15 to "preach the gospel to all creation." As he spoke these reminders to the waters, fish actually began assembling in droves, then moved closer to him, brought their heads out of the water, and "listened" diligently to him. As long as Anthony taught them, they stayed attentive. When he had first started preaching to the river the nearby group that had mocked Anthony increased their insults...until the fish phenomena took place. Then they went quiet. The fish only dispersed after Anthony blessed them, as though they were unwilling to leave until they received all that they wanted.

All in all, Anthony lived a short life. He was only 36 years old when he died. He lived fast and died young. He raised the dead and healed the sick to an unprecedented degree but died of a disease at a young age himself! How and why does this happen? We do not know, but we do know that in this hour, God wants those that carry the banner of His love to live in health, live long, and live abundantly.

In closing, it is important to add that two people were recorded to have been raised from the dead at Anthony's tomb. It seems that the resurrection power that he walked in, while not preserving his own live, still possessed the ability to defeat death in someone else's life even after he had died, not unlike the bones of Elijah.

Philip Benizi
(1223AD-1285AD)

In chapter thirteen of 2 Kings we are offered a story of a resurrection miracle that takes place at the tomb of the prophet Elisha. It is an interesting and fascinating account, covered in depth in the Appendix at the end of this book. It turns out, Elisha is not the only one whose body was used by God after death.

Oddly enough, Philip Benizi may have been used by God to raise the dead and heal the sick more after his death than when he was alive. At his funeral no less than 28 miracles broke forth including the healing of the blind, paralytics, and mental disorders. Not long after the funeral, a mother brought her daughter's mangled body to the church where Philip's body lay. Earlier that day the mother had left her daughter alone at home in the woods only to return and find a wolf devouring the girl outside the home. The child had gone outside the home and been viciously attacked. The mother fought the wolf off, scooped up what was left of her daughter, and made her way to the church.

The mother laid her daughter's body next to Philip's. The girl was raised to life, with not even a trace left over from the significant wounds that had been there only moments before.

The enemy comes to steal, kill, and destroy, but when he has, hope is not lost. God still has the answer. We can mistakenly think that all is lost when the enemy executes his plans, but that is the moment we must lean into God and believe Him to restore. In reality, the enemy has no authority. The enemy needs someone with authority (you) to agree with him in order for his plans to manifest in reality. That means that everything and anything he does is a smokescreen. In one very real sense, what he does is not real. It is our acceptance or rejection of said circumstances that determines whether the smokescreen becomes reality or if Heaven storms into our life and restores what has been stolen, killed, or destroyed.

Do not accept smokescreens; Jesus and His Kingdom are reality.

Rose of Viterbo
(1235AD-1252AD)

Rose of Viterbo is the youngest deadrasier included in this chapter. She lived in Italy, and was said to have wanted to go to church since the day she started walking. When Rose was only three years old, her aunt died. Rose went into where the body was, laid her little hands on the body, and called the aunt by name to come back to life. The aunt listened, and opened her eyes, raised to life.

The Spirit that raised Christ from the dead does not have a minimum age requirement. It isn't the faith of children that limits them from working miracles…it is the lack of faith of parents that hinders children from walking out everything God has for them. As a parent, this convicts me. The only thing holding my kids back is me! According to Jesus, children are just as capable, if not more so, to work miracles that adults.

"I tell you the truth, unless you change and become like little children, you will never enter the kingdom of heaven." -Matthew 18:3

"Then little children were brought to Jesus for him to place his hands on them and pray for them. But the disciples rebuked those who brought them. Jesus said, 'Let the little children come to me, and do not hinder them, for the kingdom of heaven belongs to such as these.'" -Matthew 19:13-14

Maybe Christ exhorts us to learn from and become like children because kids haven't been derailed by unbelief as we have; they still naturally reside in a place of imagination, faith, and creativity. Nothing is impossible to them. The unseen is just as real to them as what is seen. Studies have shown that children actually comprehend reality differently than adults. For adults, we have to learn our way back into imagination, faith, and creativity. The unlearnedness of a child is a wonderful thing to behold. Adults have rightly have grown up and learned of the natural laws and functions of the world, but children have not yet grasped these realities. As adults, our job is to rediscover the faith that we once had. It is as though we grow up and mature only to get to a point where we realize that we must go back to the start and find what we misplaced while we matured.

The first chapter of Hebrews speaks of miracles, the laying on of hands, repentance, and even the dead being raised as "elementary teachings" in Christianity. This not only means that we must adjust our definition of what is basic and introductory in Christianity, but that those that are elementary (children) are more than invited into participating in these types of activities; healing the sick, laying hands, even raising the dead.

My wife and I took this verse seriously and literally. When our first child was born, we prayed that he would raise the dead before he was five years old. He did. All it took was getting out of the way and letting God have His way. We had to consciously include our kids in situations where we would have normally gotten a babysitter. When we prayed for the sick, we brought them with us. When we prayed to raise the dead, we made sure they prayed too. Kids know a lot more than we think. They are extremely capable, and will meet the challenge if parents are willing to let them take part.

Become like a child. If you have a child, include them in the adventure. You won't regret it.

Chapter Four
(1300AD-1400AD)

.

"All the way to heaven is heaven,
because Jesus said, "I am the way."
-Catherine of Siena

Peter Armengol
(1238AD-1304AD)

Peter Armengol's life provides us with an interesting, miraculous story. Peter grew up in Spain and had a natural inclination for adventure and controversy. Thus not surprisingly, he quickly got swept up into a life of crime as can be expected for someone with such a high threshold for the rush that comes from the unexpected. People like that simply need to discover the raw thrill of following Jesus. Martyrdom, forty day fasts, heavenly encounters, traveling to unreached people groups, and boldly proclaiming the message of God's grace has more potential for heart-rushing, mind-blowing excitement than thrill seekers could ever find in leaping from planes with parachutes. Peter quickly became the leader of a gang of bandits that lived in the mountains, wreaking havoc in any situation they could.

Peter eventually gave his life to Jesus and began living out his God-given destiny instead of his self-contrived fate. Peter became a hostage negotiator. Muslims were continually capturing Christians and holding them for ransom. Peter thrived in this environment; He successfully ransomed 119 captives without any incident.

Once, when he was about to depart from a city in northern Africa and after again successfully ransoming some Christian captives from the muslims, he was given information about 18 Christian children held in a nearby prison. The muslims were mistreating them and attempting to get the children to deny Christ. Peter fulfilled one of his life goals; he made his way to the prison and offered himself in place of the children until the ransom money could be delivered to the kidnappers. The muslims agreed, and the children were set free.

Peter was resigned to martyrdom, making him even more bold than usual. Instead of peacefully waiting for the ransom money to arrive, Peter began aggressively preaching the gospel to the muslims. As a result, they began torturing Peter in hopes that he would deny Christ. After enough time had passed, the muslims grew tired of torturing him and planned to kill him. In order to get away with murder with no legal repercussions, they accused Peter of blaspheming Mohammad and being a spy that was sent by the Christian kings. Thus, the muslim population turned against him and the Saracen judge in that area ruled for Peter to be hung.

Peter, at peace with death but still knowing that there was still work to be done for the gospel on earth, prayed for God to help him. God answered his prayer. The unjust execution was carried out; Peter was hung. In the hope of dishonoring Peter and the God of the Christians, the muslims left his body hanging after the execution had been carried out so that the birds would eat Peter's remains.

A friar named Florentin had been assigned the duty of getting the money for the ransom, but Peter had already been hung by the time he got there. Heartbroken, Florentin went to the place where they had strung Peter up. Peter's body had been hanging for six days. Florentin went to get Peter down, prepared for the smell of a decomposing body. Instead he was surprised by a heavenly fragrance coming from the body. As he went to cut Peter's body down, Peter startled Florentin by suddenly speaking, declaring that God had spared his life supernaturally. In front of many witnesses, Peter was cut down and clearly alive, to the chagrin of his enemies. Many muslims in the area gave their hearts to Jesus as a result.

It is not clear from the accounts if Peter was raised back to life after dying or if his life was somehow supernaturally sustained instead. In reality, it doesn't really matter. The bottom line is that God is the carrier of abundant life; reviving, healing, and sustaining anything and everything that He gets near.

Agnes of Montepulciano
(1268AD-1317AD)

Agnes was a woman that God used to heal the sick and raise the dead in her lifetime. One such example took place while at the Chianciano baths. A child was playing by the water and regrettably fell in. Even more regrettable was that nobody noticed, including the mother. Later the body was found, to the distress of the mother. Agnes took the small body in her arms and walked away from the baths so she could pray privately. Groups of people that had come to enjoy the baths watched expectantly as Agnes walked a little ways away from them. After some time Agnes returned with the girl and laid her at her mother's feet. She then reached down and took the little girl's hand and pulled her to her feet, raised to life.

Repeatedly in researching these stories a common theme has presented itself; risk. Sometimes we can read historical testimonies and because we weren't there in person we can miss the altogether awkwardness of the moments where a woman or man steps out and risks everything in obedience to God. Think about the tenacity, the persistence, the immovableness of the actions and prayers of these men and women of God. For example, when Agnes lays the child down at the mother's feet, can you feel the unbelief in the air? Think about it; Agnes had already walked around with the child's body praying and the child had not yet been raised. The onlookers may have started feeling awkward over the fact that no miracle had taken place despite Agnes obviously praying over the child. Yet, Agnes pressed through and after laying the child down at the mother's feet proceeded to reach down, grab the child's hand, and by faith raise that child to her feet like Peter did in Acts. Notice that the girl was not raised until Agnes acted. The poor man at the gate was not healed until Peter reached out and pulled him to his feet saying, "Gold and silver I have not..."

Sometimes in our over-exulting of a godly person we miss the fact that these people took enormous risks. If you have ever stepped out in praying for healing or resurrection you can discern in these written testimonies the atmosphere of awkwardness that arises from unbelief any time someone steps out in risk and faith. In order to feel the weight of risk that these people took we have to momentarily put ourselves in their shoes. It isn't so much the working of a miracle that is the difficult part, but the willingness to be made the fool if God doesn't bail you out of the corner you have intentionally put yourself in through faith. Can you imagine the thick awkwardness that swept the room when Anthony said, "The dead man will tell you himself" in a court of law? He said that before strangers, his friends, and his family. Think about announcing something like that in front of your friends and family. Or, let us take into consideration how it felt for Stanislaus during the three day extension given by the judge wherein he was praying to raise Peter Miles after being dead for three years? Or the pressure on St. Patrick as he went in to pray for the son and daughter of the most powerful person in the country (the king)? What if you got called upon to pray for the President's children? You think there would be a bit of pressure on you in that situation? To assume that these people's faith caused them to not feel the tension of these situations is incorrect. They were humans with feelings and fears just like you and I.

Yet it must be said that when a person continually lives a life of throwing themselves at God in impossible situations they get accustomed to His faithfulness of coming through on their behalf and there is a peace that a person carries that comes from seeing the end from the beginning. That is what sets a miracle worker apart from others. They traverse situations of risk like a seasoned sea captain in a storm; while everyone else around them may be losing their mind, they calmly pilot the boat into peace and breakthrough. They aren't shaken because through faith they can see the miracle before it happens. Then, they simply call it into reality.

Faith looks like risk. Despite how uncomfortable it is, when awkwardness sweeps the room as you step out in faith you are likely right where you are supposed to be. Press through it and attain the prize.

Catherine of Vadstena
(1331AD-1381AD)

Catherine of Vadstena was princess in Sweden with a godly heritage and legacy that went before her. Catherine's mother, Bridget, also adamantly followed Jesus and has even been considered being a forerunner to the protestant reformation due to her unconventional criticism of the pope's lavish living. Bridget is reported to have raised a few people from the dead, but for now we will focus on her daughter.

Catherine is a woman that should not be forgotten simply because decades have covered up and blurred our recollection of the things God brought about through her. It is too easy to forget the wonderful things God has done; it takes intentionality to uncover them time and time again.

There was a man that was riding on top of a horse drawn coach and was employed by Catherine. Somehow he fell off and the full weight of the coach crushed him as the wheels ran over him. Catherine heard about this situation and came to the scene. The man's mangled body still lay in the same place in the street where the tragedy had happened. Catherine approached the body, took the man's hand and prayed. The man gasped, drawing in a breath of air, and was completely restored to life.

On a different occasion, a man was on a roof when he lost his balance and fell to the paved road below. Most variations of this account include the fact that this man's body was so destroyed from the fall that moving the remains was unattainable. Catherine approached the body and simply touched it. As onlookers watched, the body came back together, restored and set back into place. Bones that were broken and out of place were mended and physically ordered again, skin that had ruptured was closed and healed without scar as though nothing had ever happened, and finally, the man began stirring. He was so restored that he returned back to work the same day.

It is important to note that while instant miracles are obviously more desirable, we never know how God is going to work His will to heal and raise. It may be instantaneous or it may take time. The important thing is that once we have prayed in faith to stay in faith regardless of what our eyes behold. If we have prayed for a few hours or days it is key to not relinquish our faith through giving up. Sometimes when things do not go as we expect we can surrender our faith and dispose of the prayers we just prayed by saying things like "Well, it looks like they aren't going to be raised" or "It looks like they just wanted to stay in heaven." This is a mistake. We are too limited as human beings to assume that we know all that goes on around us in the spirit realm and what is taking place in heavenly places. Thus, if we pray in faith for something we need to follow through by simply standing after we have released what we feel God told us to release. Sometimes you are a matter of moments away from the most extraordinary miracle you have ever seen. Learn to wait on the Lord, in faith.

Catherine of Siena
(1347AD-1380AD)

Catherine of Siena was one of the two women ever to be given the honor of "Doctor" from the Catholic Church because of her ability to heal the sick and raise the dead. The other "Doctor" of the church was Teresa of Avila. The primary account of her raising the dead is as follows.

Catherine's mother Mona became sick and it was apparent that the illness would conclude in death unless God intervened. Mona had not given her heart to Jesus and this deeply concerned Catherine, so she went to her mother pleading with her to give her soul to the Lord. Mona refused and not long after, died.

Catherine was brokenhearted over the death of her mother and the thought of her mother not being in heaven. She went to her body that was about to be prepared for burial and cried out loudly to God. This was her prayer: "Lord, are these the promises you made to me? That none of my house should go to hell? Are these the things that you agreed with me about, that my mother should not be taken out of the world against her will? Now I find that she has died without repentance? By your mercy I beg you not to be let me be defrauded like this. As long as there is life in my body I shall not move from here until you have restored my mother to me."

That is what is called a "Jacob prayer". This type of desperate prayer is when a person stands firm not just against circumstances but boldly even facing God Himself, declaring that they will not let Him go until He blesses them. Only a person that knows the depths of the Lord's love and goodness can boldly approach the throne in this way. Those that are unsure about God's unwavering goodness would never have the guts to talk to a holy, sovereign, righteous King and Judge in this way. Speaking this way to God is folly outside of relationship but within the context of intimacy with God, it is beauty.

Not long later, Mona began to stir. She was raised and lived many more years until she passed at the age of 89.

Chapter Five
(1400AD-1500AD)

"Act, and God will act."
-Joan of Arc

Vincent Ferrer
(1350AD-1419AD)

Vincent Ferrer is one of the more accomplished dead raisers in history. He lived a life made of the stuff of legends, but of course the legend of his life is of the factual sort rather than mere myth.

Ferrer raised at least 28 people from the dead during his life. He was such an impressive advocate of Christ on earth that the only things contended by people about his life is not that he raised the dead, but that the reported number of people he raised from the dead is too small; many people believe that Ferrer raised many more than 28 people during his life. For the sake of brevity we will only be covering a number of the 28 resurrections, starting with a situation where a man had been condemned to death for a crime that he didn't commit. By the way the account reads, it sounds like there was a ploy instigated by a number of individuals to not only frame the man in question but also to intimidate and threaten anyone that knew what had really happened so that the truth couldn't be brought to life. Thankfully God cannot be intimidated, nor can His children.

Vincent, divinely knowing of the convicted man's innocence, pleaded with the judge for the man to be released but came up empty. As the man was escorted to the rope and noose where his doom awaited him, the courtroom procession was met by another group of people that were carrying the body of a man to the graveyard to be buried.

Addressing the dead man, Vincent suddenly said, "You no longer have anything to gain by lying. Is this man guilty? Answer me!" The dead man sat up said, "He is not!"

Vincent then asked the man if he would like to stay on the earth as a reward for his honesty. The man turned Vincent down as he had already seen heaven and knew its' beauty, laid back down on the stretcher, and passed once again.

It is wonderful that Vincent understood that it was a reward to live on the earth, even though the man that was raised did not have the wisdom to see it. In another almost identical account, Vincent asked a man the same question to which the man wisely responded that he wanted to live. Vincent responded with "Then be it so!" The man lived many more years.

Jesus did not tell us to desire to go to heaven but instead to desire for heaven to come to earth. Christ prayed, "Your will be done, your Kingdom come, on earth as it is in heaven." Rather than to die and go to heaven, our inheritance is to live and see heaven invade earth. There is no condemnation for those that get a glimpse of heaven and decide that they want to leave the earth so they can be there, but the place where we are needed is on earth, not in heaven. The mindset that desires to go to heaven rather than bring heaven to earth is one of escapism that stems from experiencing and dwelling upon the hardships of life rather than the "more than conquerors" reality that Paul spoke about. When you live in Revival (Christ), you have no need to go to heaven now because earth has become a place where God is continually present. When depression and pain lifts we begin to see this earth as a place of habitation rather than a place of affliction. When Jesus sent the disciples out, He did not pray for them to have their focus on going to heaven but instead that the Father would "not to take them out of the world, but that You would protect them from the evil one." As long as we want to go to heaven more than bring heaven to earth, we will continue to find it difficult to raise the dead because of our value for death over life.

For too long the church has thought that salvation was found in their moment of physical death rather than Christ's death 2,000 years ago. When we think that we enter heaven when we die rather than the fact that we entered heaven the day Christ died, we begin to treat death as our savior rather than Christ. We must become a people that recognize that God told us to raise the dead in Matthew 10:8 because living is our inheritance, not dying. God is a God of the living, not a God of the dead. Christ already paid for both our sickness and death. That means that we no longer need to subject ourselves to either reality. We raise the dead because death is not our portion; life is. "To die is gain" when we consider that prior to Christ our inheritance was hell and now when we die we get to go to heaven, but let us not forget that "To live is Christ". Christ is always the best choice, thus desiring to live is not less spiritual than embracing death, but more. He spent His life so you could have yours; why not honor His sacrifice by being victorious on earth rather than trying to escape by going to heaven? Your life isn't yours anyways. He bought it; Live it.

From raising the dead by simply making a sign of the cross over those that had passed to boldly calling forth the dead in a fashion reminiscent of Lazarus, Vincent actively demonstrated Christ's authority over death. In one such occasion, Vincent was preaching to a large number of people in a northwestern area of Spain when he suddenly stopped speaking and said, "Some of you go near St. Paul's gate. There you will find a dead person borne on men's shoulders on the way to the grave. Bring the corpse to me and you shall hear the proof of what I tell you."

The crowd waited as a few men went to the place of which Vincent spoke. They found a woman that had passed and was being carried to the graveyard to be buried. The men brought her body to Vincent and in front of the thousands of people there, he told the woman to come back to life. The dead woman sat up, then testified to the truth of what Vincent was claiming about the gospel. In addition the woman was able to identify who Vincent was by name, without ever meeting him prior to that moment. It seems that the dead possess information that the living do not.

Another occasion of resurrection involved a Jewish man named Abraham. Abraham was listening to Vincent but did not like what he was hearing as Vincent was declaring the divinity and holiness of Christ. Abraham got up to leave but the crowd was so dense that he wasn't able to get out. Vincent noticed and said, "Let him go! Come away all of you at once, and leave the passage free!" The moment the people backed off and let Abraham through, the passageway that the people had been blocking fell on Abraham and instantly killed him.

Vincent got up from where he was sitting and made him way over to the body. He knelt down by Abraham's body and prayed. Suddenly Abraham opened his eyes, raised back to life. The first thing out of his mouth was, "The religion of the Jews is not the true faith. The true faith is that of the Christians." Nothing is quite as evangelically effective as a man that had just been on the other side, raised from the dead.

Now for the most impressive resurrection miracle that took place in Vincent's life. At the time this story takes place, Vincent was staying with a small family while he was traveling for ministry. One night, Vincent and the father left the house to go to a nearby church where Vincent was going to speak, leaving the mother and young boy at home. The mother had a good heart but at points in the past had acted in a way that alluded to her having serious mental problems; anxiety attacks, mental breaks, etc.

The father returned from the gathering at the church to a wife that was oddly disconnected and spacey. She served him a dinner of cooked meat, but the father sensed something was awry. Looking around the house he found proof that his wife had suffered from a severe mental episode, cut their son's throat, chopped up his body, then attempted to serve the boy to the father for dinner. The horrified father fled back to the church to find Vincent. Informing Ferrer what had happened, the two of them went back to the house. Vincent proceeded to walk around the house praying as he gathered up the pieces of the child's body. Vincent then arranged the pieces in the proper order on the floor of the living room, then turned to the father. He said, "If you have faith, God, who created this little soul from nothing, can bring him back to life."

Vincent knelt and prayed, making the sign of the cross over the parts. The pieces drew together, attaching, the body drew a breath, and Vincent gave the boy back to the father, totally unharmed.

In all of history it is unlikely that a phrase is as beautiful as, "If you have faith, God, who created this little soul from nothing, can bring him back to life." Think of that moment and the devastating scene in front of you if you stood in Vincent's shoes. Yet, Vincent chose to believe. Vincent understood that God makes us from nothing, including Adam, and that it takes nothing physical and tangible to complete such a miracle. It was mere dust and dirt that God initially shaped humanity from, and it seems that all that God needs to work an incredible creative miracle is not a body that is intact, or dirt, or anything at all, but rather just a person that will believe that God is willing and capable of anything.

It is important to mention that most of the time the resurrection miracles that took place in the past were not trumpeted aloud by the people that worked the miracle. Instead, the knowledge of the miracles that took place was spread by those that witnessed them. In fact, many times the people that wrought the miracles spoke of it to no one and even asked the bystanders and witnesses of the miracle to not mention it to anyone. In this case, Vincent likely spoke of this miracle to very few if any, nonetheless, this miracle obviously gained a significant amount of public recognition as it is depicted in a painting by Francesco del Cossa in the Vatican. The location where the miracle took place is now a chapel with plaques reminding people of the reality of the supernatural occurrence that took place there.

Signs and wonders followed Vincent regularly. For example, on numerous occasions while preaching, large groups of people would witness Vincent suddenly obtain wings and literally fly off. After helping whoever was in desperate need he would return by flight to the group that he had been speaking to, land, and continue preaching as though nothing had happened.

Bernardino of Siena
(1380AD-1444AD)

Bernardino was credited with curing many lepers, preaching to crowds of 30,000, sailing over huge bodies of water on his cloak like Aladdin on his carpet, and of course, raising those that had died to life.

Once a bull was startled by a crowd and as a result, trampled and killed a young man. Bernardino went over to the body and made a sign of the cross over it saying, "By the grace of God this young man shall have no hurt! Carry him away." A few men picked the body up and began to carry it away but a few paces in, the young man sprang back up to life.

Not long after Bernardino passed away, an eleven year old died named Blasio Massei was being carried to the graveyard. As they neared the place of burial, the child suddenly sat up, raised from the dead. He told his family that Bernardino had brought him back to life, but only after sending him on an adventure. Bernardino told the child not to fear and that what he was about to experience would be used to bless many people, then little Blasio was taken on a trip through heaven and hell. Blasio experienced both the bliss of heaven and the palpable regret of hell, even becoming aware of some of the decisions people had made that resulted in them being in hell. When Blasio returned to life, he went to the families of people he saw in hell and told them to repent of specific sins that only the family knew about, blowing their minds of his knowledge about hidden things. The families repented and began to live lives that honored

God, even some of the family members selling everything and going into full-time ministry.

It may be a foreign concept for many of us to think of a person that is dead raising another person from the dead, but the Bible blurs the line between those that are alive and those that have passed just like our Catholic brothers and sisters do. Moses and Elijah, both no longer living on earth, showed up on the Mt. of Transfiguration, nonchalantly chatting with Jesus like they were out for coffee at Starbucks. A soldier was raised from the dead by the bones of Elisha, who was obviously dead. In other words, those that have passed on still have the ability to influence those us of that are living. We do not know the extent to which this is true, and we are clearly told in scripture not to consort with the dead; we also have to remember that God is the God of the living, not of the dead. God is bigger than death; He can win with any hand.

Colette of Corbie
(1381-1447)

Friends with both Vincent Ferrer and Juan Capistrano, Colette was based out of an abbey in Corbie, France. She is said to have raised many to life, including a child that had already been buried, four noblemen, a nun that was in her coffin, and numerous stillborn babies. One story involving a stillborn is as follows.

Prucet, the father, would not accept that his child was dead. He rushed the baby to the local church, where he insisted upon the little body to be baptized. The priest gently informed the father that the baby was in fact dead. Prucet walked back home, brokenhearted and distraught, holding in his arms what would have been his most prized possession aside from his wife.

Noticing his grief, Prucet's neighbors told him about Colette, who had raised the dead before and perhaps could do the same for him. His hope arising once again, Prucet quickly made his way to the monastery where Colette was. Upon seeing her, Prucet fell at Colette's feet, holding out the baby in desperation. Colette also fell to her knees, face to face with Prucet, with the baby between them. Colette began to pray and a reverence came upon the room, causing the hats to come off of the head's of those witnessing this moment of desperation, faith, and brokenness. After praying for a short time, Colette got up and removed the veil that she was wearing. She told the father to wrap the child up in the veil, then take the child to the church to get it baptized. Prucet did as Colette instructed.

When raising the dead there is usually an

uncomfortable moment of life colliding with death, usually packaged within risk and obedience. This was that moment. It is what causes some to work miracles and other not to. There is a palpable feeling of carelessness or total ignorance of what others think and in its place, a singleminded obsession with Heaven's agenda. Those that listen to the Voice can hear very little aside from It. These are the types of people that turn nations upside down, drive those that are living a compromised life absolutely crazy, and shake strongholds that have stood for centuries without even knowing it.

Despite it looking like he had lost his mind, Prucet asked the same priest to baptize the child once again. The priest, thinking of how to gently relate the unfortunate truth to the father once again, was suddenly surprised by the sound of an infant crying under the veil. Seeing that the child was alive and not knowing if the infant would continue to live, the priest frantically asked what the father wanted to name the child so that he could baptize it. The father named her Colette for obviously reasons, and she grew up to become the head nun at a monastery in Lorraine, living many years.

Joan of Arc
(1412AD-1431AD)

Joan of Arc is primarily known for her visions and military accomplishments, but it is not widely recognized that she also raised the dead. There is one occurrence of Joan praying the dead back to life but because a single resurrection is one more than most can make claim to, it should not be overlooked or omitted when considering the life of this radical, young woman.

In 1430, not long before her being burned at the stake at 19 years old, Joan went to the village of Lagny-sur-Marn. Joan became aware of a woman that had given birth to a stillborn son and was asked by some of the villagers for her to pray. Joan went to the church where the body had been laid out, finding a few young girls praying for the baby. Joan joined in and prayed as well and suddenly the child yawned three times, raised to life.

Often Joan is painted as a muscular, war-mongering shemale but in reality she was a lovesick mystic that clearly heard God's voice and happened to be stuck in the middle of a war. If the reader is wanting to discover more about Joan, the author recommends the movie "The Passion of Joan of Arc". Highly praised by movie critics, the recommendation is made not because it includes Joan's raising the child from the dead but because it was a landmark of cinema and clearly reveals Joan's absolute love and obsession with Christ. It is a beautiful and graphic account of her time in prison and subsequent martyrdom.

Francis of Paola
(1416-1507)

Francis of Paola was an Italian friar that was credited with many miracles, at least six of which were resurrections. The supernatural seems to suspend itself around Francis, regularly manifesting in a plethora of incredible ways. For example, Francis could hold burning coals without them harming him, once commanded a boulder that was rolling down a mountain to stop and it obeyed, was happy to live for six years in a cave so he could pray, and regularly healed the sick. Once, Francis needed to cross the two-mile wide strait between Italy and Sicily but had no boat. That presented no problem to Francis, as he threw his cloak down on the water, fashioned his staff into the cloak as a makeshift mast making a pseudo sail, then glided his way across the entire body of water. It gets better. Once on the other side he found the body of a convicted criminal that had been dead for three days, hung from the gallows. For reasons not known but likely out of compassion, Francis cut the body down and prayed for him to be raised to life. The criminal came back to life and fell on his knees in front of Francis, overwhelmed by gratitude. The man gave his life to Jesus and ended up being faithful to the Lord in full time ministry for many years.

Whether sheer clumsiness, demonic attack, or just bad luck, one person that Francis raised twice was first killed by a tree falling on him, then later fell off a steeple. What the man was doing standing under a tree while it was falling or hanging out on a steeple is another question altogether, but both times Francis was there and offered successful prayers of resurrection.

Once when his own nephew died, Francis had the body brought to his room so that he could pray alone. Francis continued in prayer until Nicholas was brought back to life, to the astonishment of his mother, Francis' sister. Nicholas went on to embrace the same life of ministry that his uncle had, and walked in many miracles during his life. It is one thing to pray for someone outside of your family, but things get real when what you are praying for takes place within your own family. Family is where the rubber hits the road.

In addition to the other miracles Francis worked, it is said that he also raised the son of the Baron of Belmonte, and that some whom had passed were brought back by simply laying their body next to the grave of Francis. Again, scripture attests to miracles taking place at graves, such as in the case of the Moabite raiders and the tomb of Elisha in the thirteenth chapter of 2 Kings. It is not clear why or how miracles take place at graves, and both Catholics and Protestants have their own perspective. Whatever the reason, let us not throw the baby out with the bathwater by missing the reality that however it took place, someone has been brought out of death and back into life. This is a good thing.

Francis, not unlike his same-named contemporary from Assisi, had a deep love and affection for not only humanity but for anything created, particularly animals. He lived a strict vegan lifestyle in conjunction with this affection, not only abstaining from meat but also dairy products, eggs, and other forms of protein originating from animals. It seems that his reasoning for this was not just a health based decision, but one rooted in a deep respect for living creatures. This respect led to two uncommon resurrection miracles, not having to do with humans, but animals. The first occurrence was when Francis' pet lamb named Martinello was caught and killed by workmen that had nothing else to eat. The men cooked the lamb in their lime oven and were in the process of devouring their meal when Francis approached them asked where the lamb had gone. They told him the truth, that the meat on their table was the lamb he was inquiring about. Rather than scold the men, Francis calmly asked where the leftover fleece and bones were. The men pointed to the lime kiln, still stoked and flaming, indicating that the leftovers were inside. Francis called out, "Martinelli, come out!" The lamb leapt out completely whole, unburned and unharmed, not unlike Shadrach, Meshach and Abednego. Due to its similar nature, it is possible that the testimony of this miracle later influenced Joseph of Cupertino to raise an entire flock of sheep that were killed by a hailstorm.

Another time Francis' pet trout named "Antonella" went missing. Usually when Francis came by the pond where the fish was, it would poke its head out of the water and interact with him, but on this particular day the trout was nowhere to be seen. Francis suspected that someone had caught the fish and taken it home, so he inquired around and discovered that a visiting priest was in town. Francis sent a monk to find out if the priest had taken the fish, and upon arrival discovered that he had. In addition, the fish had already been cooked and eaten. The monk asked the priest for the remains of the fish back, which infuriated the priest due to what seemed to him to be irrational and illogical. In his anger and defiance to the request he threw the remains of the fish down on the ground, breaking apart what was left of the fish. The monk gathered up the pieces and brought them to Francis. Francis put what was left of the fish back in the pond, then prayed. The parts of the fish rejoined, and the fish swam happily to the surface as though nothing had ever happened.

Miracles such as these may seem ridiculous to some. What is the point of raising a fish when there are people dying, right? The point isn't need. The point isn't its impact on eternity. The point isn't the weight of value we ascribe from our limited perspective to things that God does. God is more simple and childlike than that. The point is relationship. The point of raising a fish from the dead is not that every miracle that is worked has some grand eternal value, but that every miracle is a sign that points to God's value of relationship with us. Every miracle is a benchmark moment of God actually invading our realm with Himself. It is not the miracle or what it accomplished that really matters in the long run, but the fact that the miracle points to the undeniable reality that God was here. The impossible happening is breathtakingly beautiful because there is only One that makes the impossible possible. When the impossible does happen, it is the unavoidable proof that the same Being to craft Venus, scatter the night sky with countless planets in a matter of moments, and weave you to life in your mother's womb is intricately involved in your life.

A man had the faith to believe that every little thing matters to God, even a fish. Do you see the beautiful simplicity of that? Francis knew God well enough to know that his prayers to revive a fish, though it never really contributes anything to the Kingdom of God by swimming around in a pool, would matter to God. He knew God well enough to know that God would never mock him over something people may. He knew that God does not reason in the natural as man does. He knew that God cares about what we care about; if it matters to us, it matters to God, and the fact that Francis believed this delighted God.

Put yourself in God's shoes; virtually every person in all of history sees you for less than who you really are. We will never thoroughly grasp how wonderful and incredible He is, even after billions of centuries in heaven. Thus, if you were in God's shoes, one very real perspective is that everyone assumes the worst about you. Imagine feeling never fully understood or known, then a man comes along that believes that you are understanding, kind, and empathetic. Would you not answer his every prayer? It is not the man of faith whose prayer God answers; it is the man that knows the nature of God and gives Him the benefit of the doubt whose prayer God answers. Why? Because faith stems from the reality of knowing that God is good and nothing other than good. Faith is not the destination; it is a symptom of believing that God is good. Don't try to scrounge up faith, it won't happen. Instead, recognize how good God has been to you. The result will be faith.

Chapter Six
(1500AD-1600AD)

"You pay God a compliment
by asking great things of Him."
-Teresa of Ávila

Ignatius Loyola
(1491AD-1556AD)

Ignatius Loyola was a knight that was wounded in battle. While in recovery he decided to abandon his military life and give himself to working for the Kingdom of God. Ignatius is included in this chapter because, while he only raised one person from the dead, the details of the resurrection are not only wonderful but profoundly important as it brings up an issue that needs to be addressed; suicide.

Loyola was in Barcelona in 1524 and was passing through the street of Belloc when he heard the cries of grief and shock. Turning aside like Moses with the bush, Loyola came to find people gathered around the body a man named Lessani hanging from a rope. It quickly became clear that the man had committed suicide due to losing a lawsuit against his own brother.

Ignatius quickly cut the man down, not asking questions or pondering what the will of God was, but taking action. People attempted to revive the man through resuscitation techniques but to no avail. Ignatius prayed as he cried over the man, overwhelmed by the situation and the sorrow that he felt in his heart for Lessani. Then Ignatius stood up and spoke the name of Jesus over the body. The man opened his eyes, became conscious, and immediately repented for taking his own life, saying that it was a mistake that he now regretted.

For whatever reason, raising someone from the dead that has taken their own life has the potential to be a tender issue in the church. The reasons are many, but mainly because the question arises that if the person didn't want to live, what is the point in bringing them back? Another thought is that there are sins that God cannot overlook and thus irrevocably puts someone in a category they cannot recover from.

Some things we only regret in retrospect, after it is irreversibly done, and if we had known before doing it that it was a bad decision, most of us would likely have chosen a different path. The Bible that says that while we have all fallen short, God is capable to forgive all of our sins. While suicide is a sin, it is no greater than any other sin and it is not outside of God's forgiveness. To think that God would not want to forgive or raise someone that has taken their life, is actually adding to scripture: Christ did not say "Raise the dead unless they took their own life." Adding or taking away from what God has said in scripture will always result in folly. Whatever human reasoning is behind arbitrarily deciding that those that commit suicide are outside of God's will to be raised is in direct contradiction to Matthew 10:8. "Raise the dead" has very little exceptions; the only prerequisite being that the person must not be alive in order to qualify for a prayer to be raised from the dead. It does not say, "Raise the dead only if they are under 90 years old" or "Raise the dead if they didn't commit suicide." Nope. Lets stop trying to figure out why God won't, didn't, or can't raise the dead. Instead, lets look at God and be in awe of His power and love and in turn, think of all the reasons why He can, will, and did raise the dead. Focus on what God has done and is doing rather than what He hasn't done. In fact, that is the key to overcoming depression, which is ironic because depression is what caused Lessani to hang himself.

For some reasons, as humans we are always looking

for reasons for good things not to happen. This is the case when it comes to dead raising, and especially in situations where someone has taken their own life. We think of reasons why people shouldn't be, or aren't, raised. We reason with our limited knowledge, things become thoroughly complicated, new doctrines arise, and before we know it, we have talked ourselves right out of faith rather than just accepting the fact that "Nothing is impossible with God". The Kingdom of God does not function through man's logic, reason, or formulas. He doesn't think the way we do. Instead, the Kingdom of God is mysteriously wonderful, pervasively simple, and always driven by love in its purest form. The Kingdom of God is the domain of a living, glorious King. When you are within it, you want not. When you are surrounded by it, everything works.

Some people have a distorted idea of man's free will and the role it plays in God affecting His will in a situation. We have free will; that is a fact. But remember that sometimes our free will can get hijacked by demonic powers. When this happens a person becomes confused and accepts what is wrong to be right. There are people all around us that are mentally afflicted by both chemical imbalances in their brain and demonic powers. To think that a person in that state, who chooses to take their own life, cannot be raised because they have used their free will to bring about their own death is settling for less than what Jesus paid for. While people's free will play a part in the Kingdom of God taking over this earth, God's will is still greater. God's grace is bigger. God's love is better. God is so creative and knowledgeable that He has a way of bringing about His will without violating anyone else's. If someone you know or hear about takes their own life, do not let doubt derail you in your conviction that they should live. Nothing is impossible with God, even when people, in the power of their own free will, make bad decisions.

Why raise someone that killed themselves? Some decisions you don't regret until it's too late to change it. It is fact that someone that kills themselves and did not know Jesus will find themselves in a place much, much worse than earth. If they thought that they were depressed here, it did not compare to the utter privation of that place. Earth is heaven to those in hell; Raise them back and lead them to Jesus.

Peter of Alcantara
(1499AD-1562AD)

Peter of Alcantara lived in Spain and Portugal and was the spiritual counselor to Teresa of Avila, who is covered more in depth later on in this chapter. When in prayer, Peter regularly experienced ecstasies where bystanders would witness beams of light shooting forth from his body. He was also known to lift into the air during prayer and rest there, suspended in the air. In a few situations it is said that he literally took flight, shooting up to a cross fixed on a roof so that he could embrace it as he prayed. Teresa of Avila, wherein whose biography we learn the little we know about Peter, said that Peter would eat and sleep rarely, regularly eating only once a week and sleeping on average only an hour a night, sitting up. Due to the lack of information on Peter's life, of the six people that he raised, we only have detailed information about one of them.

In 1556 the son of the Count of Osorna became very sick. The Count had deep respect and adoration for Peter, and asked if he would come pray for his son. Peter obliged, but by the time he made it to the son's bedside, the son of the Count had already passed. Peter was distraught. After a short time of prayer, Peter got up and threw himself on the body, not unlike Elijah did with the widow's son. He remained in this position for quite some time, totally immovable, in prayer. Time passed. Peter continued to pray. The body was said to have been colder than marble when Peter started, but when it started to grow warm again, Peter drew himself off the body as the young man suddenly stretched, then opened his eyes. The boy stood up as the Count and all that were present began wildly yelling, "A miracle! A miracle!" The young man ran to Peter and began to thank him, as on the other side he had been aware that it was a "supernatural light" that had saved him, and knew that it was in connection with Peter's prayers.

Have you ever prayed to raise the dead? If you have, have you held such conviction, such awareness of the family's grief and loss that you thought not about throwing your body on the body of someone that has died, and declaring prayers of life into the face of the person who is dead? It isn't the laying on the body that brings the miracle; no formula will always work. Instead, it is the heart of a person willing to follow Jesus in any way He seems fit, the person that cares not how he looks because he is too connected to and aware of the destitution of the family, that works miracles. It is the person that can possess love so deeply in their heart, spirit, and mind that no fear of man can have even an ounce of them. It is the person whose focus and singularity of vision is Jesus that wins back to life those that are dead. Be a lover of God.

Sebastian of Apparizio
(1502AD-1600AD)

Sebastian of Apparizio was born a Spainard, but became a missionary to Mexico early on in his life. Sebastian walked in the miraculous during his life, such as his ability to supernaturally produce wine when it had run out. Sebastian never raised the dead while he was alive, but is included in this chapter because he was still credited with six resurrections, though all of them took place after his death.

That may sound odd to anyone with a Protestant leaning, but let us remember that even in the Bible, those that had passed on raised the dead. Of course it is God that raises the dead, but to say that Elisha's bones had nothing to do with the miracle of the dead soldier coming back to life after touching the prophet's bones in 2 Kings 13 would be misled. The real question is the "why?"

In reality, we do not know. The supernatural is not a science that we can consistently measure, rationally understand, or logically critique. God's ways are different than ours, and to attempt to tack down a formula as to how He works will only result in the need to reevaluate it when God works in a way that is different from what we expected. We don't always know the "why", but we do know He is good. That is as much as a formula as we need; He is always good.

While we cannot say exactly how and why miracles happen, we do know a few things. First, something about Elisha's bones brought a dead man to life. It is likely that there was a residue of the Spirit of God on that buried body, just like there was a substance or remnant of the

Spirit of God on the handkerchief and aprons that healed the sick in Acts 19. Let us not limit our wonderful Counselor, the mighty Spirit of God, by assuming that when His manifest Presence lifts there is not something leftover. Not unlike honey, He is thick and sweet and hard to pull off of something without leaving some sweetness behind. It is likely that the time that Elisha spent in the Presence of God resulted in even his bones being anointed with resurrection life.

Before we delve into the stories from Sebastian's life, or rather, from his life after life, it is important for us to understand that Jesus is the only One we need. He is our great Intercessor and the One we fix our eyes upon. We have no real need to pray to Mary, or a saint, or anyone else. There are many times in history when people have prayed to "saints" and the miracle they were believing for took place. But we do not have the liberty to throw out or discredit these miracles just because they don't fit in or mesh with Protestant thinking or theology. Instead, let us seek to understand.

That brings us back to the first question; Why do these miracles happen when someone prays to someone other than God? Because God is merciful and full of grace. As humans, we have a hard time relating to an invisible, perfect, wonderful God. For some people, usually Catholics, it seems it is easier for them to relate to a person that has passed on that lived a godly life than God Himself. And while this is actually settling for less than what God has for us, not unlike God's people choosing to have a king rather than talk to God themselves (1 Sam. 8-12), God is gracious.

The incarnation is a bewildering, incredible, life-changing reality. The fact that God came and became a man, let alone a little baby, will forever be a point of worship for all of eternity. It is not only God saying to humanity, "I choose to trust you", but it is the most vulnerable, intimate thing God has ever done. God becoming a man is like a man becoming an ant, but on a scale millions of times greater.

Ants do not understand men. Ants only understand ants. The idea of sleeping in a bed, or taking your children to swimming lessons, or the feeling of pride that comes as you embrace your child after they tie their shoes on their own for the first time is utterly foreign to an ant; they have no way of empathizing with our lives in the least bit. The only way a person could even remotely communicate to ants is to become an ant.

So Christ did. He became a man; a preverbal ant. He did this so that we could, sometimes only a moment, grasp the height, depth, and width of the love that God has for us. His love is otherworldly to us, beyond all comprehension, and we still have yet to discover even the tip of the iceberg of the love of God. In fact, until Christ came and still after, humanity had and has an inherent belief that God possesses some sort of vendetta against humanity rather than unconditional love. Our fallen state is most on display not by our stumbling and sin, but by the way that across the board, humanity assumes the worst of God until Holy Spirit illuminates our thinking through revelation. Most of the time, even after Christ came and revealed to us a perfect representation of God the Father (Heb. 1:3), men still think of God as angry, judgmental, wrathful, critical, and demanding. Most of us have all sorts of ways of defining God aside from how Paul defined God; "God is love."

Thus it is not a surprise that when a desperate mother

and father lost their son because a horse kicked him in his head that they resorted to the only thing they really knew; praying to a godly man that they knew did miracles, but had now passed on to the cloud of witnesses. Maybe, they thought in their desperation and sadness, he would hear our prayer even if God did not. And being that God is gracious, hard to offend, and willing to receive even misguided faith as long as it is faith in something or someone, Giovanni and Maria quickly found their beloved son completely restored, even though he had been dead for an hour. He was so completely healed that the child went back to playing with his friends soon after being raised.

Once, a child accidentally fell out of a window and landed on a pile of rocks below. The mother took his body to her mistress, who began to pray for the child, asking for Sebastian to work a miracle on their behalf. She got ahold of a piece of Sebastian's garb and laid it on the child's chest, then wrapped the body in a sheet. Four hours later the child suddenly sat up and asked for something to eat.

On another occasion, an infant somehow fell into a stream that made its way under several houses. Quickly the child disappeared from sight and when the family finally found the child, she had long since passed. The little girl's parents prayed to Sebastian, asking for his help. The child was raised, perfectly healthy.

Once, the parents of a baby girl that especially adored Sebastian lost their daughter to sickness. Somehow they had come into ownership of one of Sebastian's personal possessions and laid it on the chest of the child. Again, a mother received back her dead child to life.

Another time, a child got lost outside and was later

found frozen to death. Those that were there tried their best to warm her body up and then resuscitate her, but to no avail. Her body was prepared for burial by being wrapped up, then a lady named Donna Francesca took a portion of Sebastian's garb and placed it on the child's body. The little girl suddenly warmed and began to breath, raised and restored.

If the message of the goodness of God does not precede the message of what God can do, the result will always be people drawing closer to people rather than Him. When we don't realize that everything He does is good we tend to elevate good people rather than Christ. So the next time someone prays to Mary or St. Francis rather than Christ, instead of it offending us let it be an indicator to us of someone's need to further understand the goodness, the incredible approachableness, the kindness of God. He is not far away from and disassociated with our lives. He is near, and He is good.

Francis Xavier
(1506AD-1552AD)

Francis of Xavier lived during the same era as Sebastian of Apparizio as well as during the undertaking and implication of the Reformation with Martin Luther. Born in Spain and commissioned to Asia as a missionary, Francis was extremely effective and fruitful in the East. Hailed as one of the greatest missionaries of all time, some believe that only Apostle Paul was greater than Francis in bringing the gospel to foreign lands. Francis secured hundreds of thousands of people into the Kingdom, baptized 100,000 by his own hand, and worked countless miracles in under ten years of ministry. He did all of this in such a short amount of time without the traveling conveniences that we have today, such as the abundant use of cars and planes. Sometimes the boat rides he would take lasted longer than a year, one way. Francis used the amount of time leftover (after subtracting how long it took to travel everywhere) so proficiently that the world will never be the same. This is a man we would be wise to imitate.

Francis' first resurrection took place in Coimbatore, India. Francis was about to start a church service when a crowd of people entered, carrying the body of a young boy. The boy, whom Francis had baptized himself, had fallen in a well and drowned. Francis didn't skip a beat; he began to pray, took the boy by the hand, and commanded the boy to rise. The child did as he was told and then ran to his mother. Go Jesus.

On another occasion, Francis was being accompanied by two younger men on a missionary journey. During the night one of the men was bit on the foot by a snake. Whether the man slept through the bite or simply did not alert Francis is not clear; what is known is that when Francis awoke, the man was dead. Francis spit on the man's foot, prayed over him, and suddenly pulled him to his feet. It is said that the man was raised as simply as if he had been napping. He continued escorting Francis on the missionary journey, in perfect health.

The Bible communicates many promises that God has made to us. One such promise is in Mark 16:18 where Jesus tells us that even snake venom will not have authority over the bodies of His followers. Thus, when someone dies from a snake bite, why would we surrender that promise and not stake a claim to it? What is it about death that deters so many from what is legally theirs through Christ? The prayer for resurrection is beautiful because it is the boldface declaration that God is not a liar and that it is not time to give up, but lean into God even more. The prayer of resurrection shakes the very foundations of hell by its joyful expectancy of light. God has promised us healing of all sickness, thus when someone dies from sickness, what about that situation would cause us to believe that God has relinquished His promise to heal all sickness? At that point, it is time more than ever to continue to stand in faith on the promises of God and call that which is not as though it were. Death is a defeated foe; we cannot buy into its smokescreen when it raises its head. It is not over when someone dies.

Another time in Multan, now a large city in Pakistan, Francis came across a funeral procession carrying the body of a young man that had died from a fever. He had been wrapped in a burial shroud for twenty-four hours, but this did not deter Francis. He knelt down, looked to

Heaven, then prayed. He sprinkled the young man's body with water he had blessed, then ordered those carrying the body to cut open the funeral shroud. Once the body was out of the wrappings, Francis prayed over the boy again, then took him by the hand and told the boy to live. The entire crowd watched as the boy came to life and was given back to his mother and father. In commemoration of what God had done, a great cross was erected in that spot and a festival of celebration took place that night to thank God for what He had done.

Once when on the coast of India, across Palk Strait from Sri Lanka, Francis ran into extreme hardheartedness in those that he preached to. Rather than giving in and letting them win, Francis took it up a notch and stopped to pray. Suddenly he directed a few of the young men nearby to go open the nearby grave of a man that had been buried the day before. He then told the crowd that God was pleased to even raise the dead in their presence in order that they would give their lives to Jesus.

When the young men opened the tomb, likely due to the heat that is typical of southern India, a distinct stench filled the air that indicated the overwhelming reality of a body that was already decaying. Francis actually brought attention to this fact, telling everyone there to pay attention to the fact that the body was undeniably rotting. When God is going to do a miracle, it is wisdom to bring attention to the problem, otherwise those that lack faith will claim in retrospect that there was never a problem to begin with. One of the most clear indicators of doubt is the questioning afterwards if there was ever a problem to begin with. Francis prayed over the decomposing body and the man sat up, alive. The text says, "in perfect health". The crowd fell at Francis' feet, and many were baptized that day. This resurrection miracle and the one preceding before it, together were the main reason for most of the entire kingdom in that region to give themselves to Jesus. Back then, word traveled quickly when someone was raised from the dead.

On another occasion, reminiscent of Lazarus' story, a mother came to Francis with the request that he would come and pray for her daughter to be raised from the dead. She had seen him heal the sick and reasoned that if Francis could do that, surely he could also raise the dead. While listening to her, Francis' heart was deeply moved. He turned to her and said that she should go to the grave where her daughter was buried, for she was alive. It was then that the mother revealed that her daughter had been dead and buried for three days, but Francis didn't bat an eye over this fact. The mother took note of Francis' confidence, and in a sprint of hopeful faith she ran to the church where her daughter had been buried. The tomb was sealed off by stone but with the help of those that had accompanied her to the church, they managed to lift it off the tomb to reveal the contents inside. Out crawled her daughter, raised from the dead and totally restored.

Once, in Japan near Kagoshima, there was a father that lost his only daughter. He was advised by friends to go to Francis and see if he could do anything for the father in his broken state. The father took their advice and found Francis, then threw himself at his feet. The father was so distraught that he couldn't speak, but simply wept there, crumpled up on the ground. Taking some time to pray with Joam Fernandez, the man accompanying him, Francis told the father to leave; that the father's prayers had been heard by God. Not hearing faith but rejection and emptiness, the father turned to head back home, completely broken and overcome by grief. While on his walk back home, the father was met by one of his servants who joyfully informed him that his daughter was alive. Not long after that, his daughter met him on the road herself, throwing herself into her father's arms. They rejoiced together, then the daughter recounted what had happened to her when she had died. When she breathed her last, she suddenly found herself being escorted to hell by two demons. They were about to throw her into this place of ruin when two men suddenly came to her rescue and escorted her back out of the darkness. When the father brought her to Francis' house, she immediately identified Francis and Joam as the two men she was rescued by.

Did you know you can be a hero? People are dying all around us, and God has given us the ability to actually save people from the fires of hell through the power of prayer! Resurrection is beautiful because it is the Saving Arm of God even in situations that seem irreversible and eternal. God's arm is strong enough to pull those out of the mire that have sank deep into it!

Another time when Francis was sailing on the Santa Croce to China with the destination of Changchun, a five year old boy fell overboard. The ship had recently caught a very strong gust of wind and was traveling at a considerable speed, and by the time the father of the child noticed that he had gone overboard, the idea of rescue was out of reach, if not totally impossible. They had to watch as the child struggled in the water, quickly being left behind and eventually drifting out of sight. For three whole days, the poor father was in deep despair. On the third day Francis happened to run into the father on the deck and learned of his child going overboard three days before. Somehow, Francis had not heard of the news until this point. Francis asked the father if he would receive Christ in the case that God restored his child to him. The father quickly said that he would. A few hours passed, assumedly while Francis prayed. Suddenly, as the father stood on the deck, the child came running to him. They embraced, both bewildered and overcome by the love and care of God. The father stayed true to his word and gave his life to Christ.

There are a few more accounts where Francis raised people, one being a woman that had been dead for a whole day and another being a young man named Francis Ciavos, who became a monk as a result of his being raised from the dead.

Teresa of Ávila
(1515AD-1582AD)

One of the most distinct authorities on prayer, Teresa of Ávila not only led countless into understanding union with God and experiencing ecstasy in prayer, but she also raised the dead at least once, possibly more.

Teresa's own sister was the mother of a six year old named Gonzalo. At the time when this story took place, Juana was also pregnant. One night, Juana, her husband, and Teresa decided to go out and leave Gonzalo home alone. Unfortunately, upon returning back home, Juana's husband found Gonzalo dead, laying on the floor. Juana had not yet seen the body, and Teresa wanted to do everything she could to protect the unborn baby, so she told a person nearby to keep her sister occupied while she went to pray for the child. Juana's husband tried his best to resuscitate the boy, but to no avail.

Now it was Teresa's turn. She cradled the boy in her arms and covered his face with her veil as she prayed for God to spare the parents of the sadness that would overtake them if their child stayed dead. Teresa knew that grief of such significance and depth would not only distort the parent's lives forever, but could also affect the unborn baby to a fatal degree. At that moment, Juana walked into the room, saw Teresa cradling the body, and asked what was going on. Teresa simply motioned for her sister to stay calm in a nonchalant way, as though nothing was wrong at all. At that moment, the boy began to breathe and reached out and touched Teresa's face.

The kind of steadfastness that a person needs when bringing the Kingdom of God into the lives of family members is far greater than when bringing the Kingdom of God to people that they do not know. There is some sort of unfortunate truth about familiarity bringing contempt; it isn't guaranteed, but is likely. When we lose our ability to recognize the anointing, specifically the anointing, in another person that we are familiar with, we have settled for a perspective of them that is unlike God's. It is very easy to do.

There is something about being able to minister to one's own family as opposed to ministering to people that you do not know or know very little. Ministering to one's own family assumes that a person, when out of the spotlight, lives the same life behind the scenes that they live when in the public's eye. When a family can receive ministry from another person in the family it shows us that the family does not see hypocrisy in the life of the one ministering, and as a result, willingly receives from the person.

Let us be people like Teresa that, for the sake of those we love the most, do not live even a fraction of a double life. This way, those we love may be able to receive from us when bad times try to rush upon us.

Philip Neri
(1515AD-1595AD)

Philip Neri was considered an apostle to Rome and while he healed many with a simple touch of his hand, he also raised the dead.

Once, a teenager named Paolo that Philip had known since birth grew very sick, laying on his bed for months with a dangerous fever. Philip regularly visited him and prayed for him. One day the 14 year old suddenly grew much worse, and someone went to inform Philip that Paolo was going to die. The messenger found that Philip was in Mass and wasn't to be interrupted. By the time Philip got out of Mass, was informed of the situation, and made his way to Paolo's bedside, the youth had already passed. Philip prayed for a short time as both his heart and body shook, then took some water and sprinkled it on the boy's face. He let some water drip off his finger into the boy's mouth, then breathed on his face, then laid his hand on Paolo's forehead. Suddenly in a loud voice, Philip called out, "Paolo! Paolo!" At Philip's words, Paolo returned to life.

This story is a teaching lesson to all of us because of the persistence that Philip demonstrated in prayer. Philip's prayer wasn't striving but a continual steadiness that did not waver, even when death entered the picture.

Sometimes when we have been praying for healing for an extended amount of time, it start to feel familiar. Sometimes we have been praying for someone's healing for weeks, months, sometimes years, and this can make it very difficult to believe for resurrection if they die from the illness because of the natural reasoning of the minds of men. We logically rationalize that if we couldn't get them healed of a sickness after all of this time and prayer, then how can we get them raised? We must remember that to God, no miracle takes more effort than another; healing a headache and raising the dead are no different to Him, and neither is more difficult for Him to pull off. They are on par in His mind; it is our mindset that needs to shift and begin to think like He does.

If a person that we have been praying healing for passes after all of that prayer, should we not continue to pray? Death's greatest power is not the ability to take life, but intimidate us into thinking that it does. Death is a defeated foe. When someone dies after prayer has already been given on their behalf for months and years, instead of backing off or feeling intimidated, stand your ground and simply shift from declaring healing to declaring life. Continue to pray.

Louis Bertrand
(1526AD-1581AD)

Louis Bertrand was a Spainard that was sent to South America as a missionary. His success in both bringing the Kingdom of God wherever he went as well as raising those that had passed was nothing short of exceptional. There are biographies and various historical sources that convey that Louis raised a least fifteen people from the dead.

For example, in a port in Cartagena, Columbia a woman died and Louis showed up, offered prayer, and raised the woman back. In another circumstance he laid his prayer beads on a dead woman and she was restored. There are numerous stories like this pertaining to Louis' life, and his ability to win souls and work miracles was evident to those that he came in contact with.

Sometimes people wonder why they haven't raised the dead when others have raised the dead on multiple occasions. Other questions people ask are why it seems that God raises the dead overseas so much or did in the past more than He does now. All of those questions assume that the people that raised the dead in the past or overseas live the same lives as the people asking the questions. The fact of the matter is that God is the same today, yesterday, and forever. God is the same whether you are in Africa or America. God is the same now as He was in the 1500s or who He will be in 2050. The fact of the matter is that Louis lived his life in a way that was radically different than most people of his day, or our day. He raised the dead because he was a man of continual prayer and ministry. He continually prayed for the dead to be raised. Many times the people that are asking those types of questions have never even prayed in person to raise the dead. Louis made himself available to men and to God continually, and those realities made raising the dead something that took place in his life over a dozen times.

Just think: Louis wanted souls so badly that he made the long and dangerous journey across the ocean only a handful of years after the New World (the West/Americas) was discovered. He was undeterred by the danger and risk in going; He only wanted the Kingdom to come.

What if we laid down our lives like Louis and the other deadraisers that went before us? If we would, we would see the same things that they saw because God is the same God to us that He was to them. Let us love Jesus to such a sold-out, radical degree that there is no risk we would not take to see Him glorified.

Chapter Seven
(1600AD-1900AD)

"Listen to the sermon preached to you by the flowers, the trees, the shrubs, the sky, and the whole world. Notice how they preach to you a sermon full of love, of praise of God, and how they invite you to glorify the sublimity of that sovereign Artist who has given them being."
-Paul of the Cross

Mariane de Jesus of Quito
(1618AD-1645AD)

Mariana of Quito was another New World deadraiser and lover of God. When her niece was kicked in the head by a mule, collapsing the skull and killing her with the blow, Mariana had the child brought to her room where she prayed over her. The child was brought back to life and had no mental or physical issues whatsoever.

Another time Mariana was in prayer and saw a vision of a man killing his wife through strangulation. She watched as he threw her body over a cliff in hopes of hiding the body. When Mariana came out of the vision she asked a man that she knew to go to the location of where the body had been disposed and bring the body back to her. The man did as she asked; upon arriving at the indicated location he climbed down the steep slope and found a woman's body at the bottom. In secret he brought the body back to Mariana, who brought the body into her quarters and began to pray. The woman was raised back to life, completely undoing the evil plans of the husband.

Man makes plans of evil but God is bigger. When we tap into the Voice of the Lord and He begins to reveal to us that He wants to change, we can shift the circumstances dramatically. God wants to invade society and bring His Kingdom into every genre of life, even the correctional and judicial system. There is an hour coming where people will be given the locations of missing people, dead or alive, and God will intervene as they step out. There is incredible evil in the world, but God's love is bigger.

Imagine it: Underground human trafficking being ended through words of knowledge. Police stations partnering with churches because the prophetic people in the churches are so consistently seeing pictures of where kidnapped children are being kept that it would be folly not to listen to them. Paramedics being promoted and honored because their prayers resulted in more lives saved than any other ambulance workers in the area. When the Kingdom of God is more established in our societies, the outcome will be life and life abundant; the possibilities are endless.

Francis of Jerome
(1642AD-1716AD)

Francis of Jerome lived and ministered in Naples, preaching in fields to crowds of 10,000 people each sermon. Many miraculous things happened in addition to him raising the dead; fishermen would pull in incredible catches after he prayed for them, a lava flow from Mt. Vesuvius stopped in its tracks after he prayed, and many were healed. On more than one occasion people tried to interrupt Francis' speaking by leading oxen and horses into the middle of the listening crowd but were surprised when their animals simply stopped and bowed to Francis, standing still and quiet in reverence.

Francis once prayed for a man that was a well-known physician in Naples. He had been sick and Francis had been sent for, but by the time Francis arrived, the man had already expired. After some time of reciting some prayers, suddenly Francis stood up and declared three times, "Pompey, in the name of Jesus Christ, I command you to answer me!" On the third declaration, the man opened his eyes and asked, "What do you want with me?" Francis responded, "We want you to remain with us." The doctor did so, perfectly healthy.

On another occasion, Francis told a woman named Marie to go to his confessional where she would find a child "sleeping". As in Christ's situation with Lazarus wherein Jesus said that Lazarus was only sleeping when He was aware that he was quite dead, Francis also took this perspective. Maybe Jesus and Francis did this to instill hope into those nearby; to convey that raising the dead is as easy for God to pull off as it is to wake someone from a nap. Marie went to the confessional and just as Francis had said, there lay a little girl, wrapped in a burial shroud, stiff, with skin that was white and cold. Marie clarified with Francis that the child was in fact dead, but Francis disagreed, and told Marie to cut the burial shroud away. Francis stroked the child's face and called out the name "Teresella!". The little eyes opened, the body became pliable, and the skin that had been bone white began to become pink again. Francis turned to Marie, smirked and said, "Did I not tell you that she was only asleep?" They gave the child water, then Francis told Marie to put the child back in the confessional, then to look for a veiled woman nearby and tell her to come to him. Marie did as he asked, and the mother came to Francis wondering what he wanted. Francis asked her, "Why did you not take your child with you when you left the confessional?" The mother replied that she had no children, so Francis said, "Go back to the confessional and see whether it is true or not that you do not have a child." When the mother opened the confessional, her daughter reached out her arms saying, "Mama! Mama!" The mother went back to Francis, weeping, and communicated that she was a widow and had no money for a proper burial, so she left her daughter's body in the confessional hoping that they would give her a Christian burial. Francis gave her some money and sent her on her way, happy and whole.

The Bible says things like, "Why would you consider it incredible that God would raise the dead" (Acts 26:8). Hebrews 6 states that the resurrection of the dead is an "elementary teaching". Over and over again the authors of the Bible are communicating the revelation that dead raising doesn't need to be seen as amazing, that nothing is impossible with God, and that we should not let anything intimidate us, downgrade our faith, or overcome us. Jesus chose to see Lazarus as asleep despite knowing he was dead because it is actually more realistic and congruent to view someone as needing to be woke from a nap than needing to be raised from the dead. Anyone can wake someone from a nap. Nobody wonders how to wake someone up; you just do it. It is elementary; even a child can wake someone up from a nap. The same is true with resurrection. You can do it. It is simple. You already know how. Just go do it.

Paul of The Cross
(1694AD-1775AD)

Paul of the Cross was a mystic that had many encounters with Jesus during his time on earth. As typical of a mystic, Paul also claimed to have been visited by people that had died and gone to a place of waiting, testifying of how awful it was to not find themselves in heaven after death.

One of the first time Paul raised the dead happened when he was attempting to convert some soldiers. They were resistant to the message and even mocking Paul. One of soldiers pointed to a partially butchered cow nearby and arrogantly said, "I will be as soon converted as that ox returns again to life!"

At that moment, the ox came back to life and charged with rage at the solider, slamming into the spot the man had been sitting just a moment before before he leapt out of the way. The ox died again from the hit, but the solider was true to his word and gave his heart to Jesus.

Once in 1741 a child was in a window watching a crowd leaving the church. He managed to accidentally fall out of the window, landed on paved ground, and was killed instantly. The called on doctors but when they arrived, it was clear that the boy was without life.

About that time, Paul was somewhere else about to board a boat to go to another place. The parents of the child ran to find Paul and moments before they shipped out, they ran up to him and told him what had happened to their child. Paul went with them back to the body.

Upon seeing the body, Paul went quiet for quite some time. After his silence, Paul spread his hands over the body. Within a few seconds, life returned to the child and he handed the child to his parents, alive and well.

On a few occasions, Paul raised back to life animals that had been killed. One example was when a chicken was served for dinner, fully cooked. Paul was grateful for the meal, but knew by a word of knowledge that the chicken had provided for a widow nearby by continually laying eggs for her to eat. He told his host what the Lord had showed him, then asked his host to open the window. He then blessed the animal and the moment he did, the hen came back to life, sprouted feathers, and took off flying out the window and back to the woman.

Once a person gets a taste for abundant life, nobody is exempt. Human or animal makes no difference. All of creation waits for the sons of God to be revealed on the earth, to step into their inheritance of life and life abundant. The earth is groaning, writhing, waiting for us to come declare life back to her. When raising the dead is limited to humans, we have somewhat lost the point of the restorative work that Christ intends to do on the earth. He will restore everything.

In Acts 3:21, Peter uses the wonderful greek word "apokatastasis" when referring to all things. We commonly translate this word to mean restitution or restoration. Peter is letting us into a fabulous truth; that through the Church God will eventually restore all things. He will not only restore humanity, but the entire earth. At the cross, the Church was passed the baton and we will see it come about!

Any time there is death, it is a violation of the order of heaven. Any time there is sickness, it is a violation of the way the earth and it's inhabitants are supposed to live. Any time there is corruption, it is a violation of the way things are intended to be. We are to call the earth and everything on it back to it's original inheritance of life and life abundant. We were initially created in a corruptionless, sinless, deathless, sickless world where we would walk in the cool of the day with God Himself, and we **will** get back to that reality.

John Bosco
(1815AD-1888AD)

John Bosco is a more modern day resurrector of the deceased. He and a handful of other Catholic priests such as Padre Pio were well known for making that which was usually extraordinary ordinary. In 1849, a fifteen year old named Charles was close to death due to an illness. He requested John Bosco to come and pray for him, but John was out of town. The young man had already passed when John finally returned home, but when told of the boy's state, John responded not unlike Christ when hearing of Lazarus' passing; "He is just asleep." John was assured that the young man was in fact dead, that the whole family knew it, and that the death certificate had already been signed. John held his ground and requested to be taken to the body. Once in the room with the boy, John had everyone else leave the room except the mother and an aunt. The body was covered with a burial shroud, sewn around it. John closed the door, prayed for a short time, then declared, "Charles! Rise!" The body under the sheet began to stir as the mother and aunt watched. John tore the sheet away and got the young man's head uncovered. Charles sighed, asked why he was dressed in a shroud, then noticed John and was clearly excited that his hero was there as he had requested. The entire family flooded into the room to greet Charles in great joy.

In 1866, John was in Florence and came across a boy that lay dead. John began to pray, then others with him began to pray as well. The boy began to breathe, raised to life.

People die every day. What if the Church, 2 billion

strong, actually began to exemplify the victory over death that they carry in their bones? Inside us dwells the same Spirit that raised Christ from the dead. Let us keep our eyes and ears open for moments where not only can God be glorified by someone being raised, but a loved one be returned to a grieving family. Oh the pain God has spared us from by the gift of life He secured us through His own on the cross. By His wounds we are healed, raised, and restored.

Chapter Eight
(1900-1950)

"The resurrection of Jesus Christ is the greatest event in human history, without any doubt."
-John G. Lake

Smith Wigglesworth
(1859-1947)

Known as the apostle of faith, few can compare to Smith Wigglesworth in obedience, unwavering belief, and healing the sick. Doing exactly as Holy Spirit led despite it being controversial sometimes, Wigglesworth raised numerous people from the dead. As many as twenty-three people were raised during Smith's life. What follows are a few of those accounts.

Once, Smith was called to the bedside of a woman ridden with tumors. The woman had a daughter who was young and blind. When Smith saw the mother and child, his heart broke, not only over the mother's state but over the child's vulnerable state, especially if her mother died. Smith asked the mother, "Do you want to live?" The mother was so ill that she could not verbally respond but she lifted one of her fingers to show that she wanted to live. Smith anointed her with oil and prayed in the name of Jesus for her but not long after the woman passed nonetheless. Smith felt the resurrection power that comes with compassion, picked up the woman's body and carried her across the room. Smith then held the corpse up against a wardrobe and commanded her to walk. The body fell hard to the floor and undeterred, he picked her up again and commanded death to leave and for her to walk. The body began to shake like a leaf and he told her to walk once again. She did. Later a doctor wanted to confirm this story so he went and found the woman in question. She was alive and in health and told the story exactly how Smith had, but added her perspective which was from heaven, confirming that she had been dead and out of the body.

Another time, Smith was requested to come and pray for a young person that the doctor had given up on. Tuberculosis had taken its toll on this young woman and when Smith arrived, he realized the situation was much worse than he had understood previously. It was clear that unless God did something, the young woman would die very soon. The family was present, but Smith was disappointed by the sympathy and unbelief coming from the family members rather than faith, so he suggested that everyone go to bed and in doing so, leave the room. The family resisted Smith's suggestion so he grabbed his coat, readying himself to leave. Smith understood that we must create a place of faith, a place of invitation of the will of God, in order for the Spirit of God to do what He wanted to do. While God can work in the atmosphere of unbelief through sheer grace, it is still not the most conducive atmosphere to bringing forth God's will in a situation; Faith is always better. Smith knew that even the Lord had the mourners put out of the room because while grief and mourning are understandable, they do not mesh with the spirit of faith. Grief and mourning are the acceptance and processing that something bad has happened, but faith is the exact opposite; Faith does not idly accept that something bad has taken place and stands its ground until things shift bad into good. When the family realized that Smith was planning on leaving if they did not go to bed, they relented and headed to bed. Smith fell to his knees and began to pray. For some time it was intense. God encouraged Smith and put strength in him, and then the fight became especially intense. Smith said that the heavens felt like brass. For four hours he prayed. Around 3am he watched the young woman's spirit leave her body.

She stopped breathing and died. Most of us would give up at this point but Smith is not like most people; instead of giving up, he simply switched from offering prayer for the sick to be healed to offering prayer for the dead to be raised. He continued praying and allowing God to strengthen his faith. After some time, Smith looked up and saw the face of Jesus in the window. He said it looked like a million rays of light were coming from His face. The face of Christ turned and looked upon the girl. Suddenly she rolled over and went to sleep, raised from the dead. Smith rejoiced, then left. The family said that the next morning the girl got up, put on a dress, and walked over to the piano. She played a beautiful song and thanked God for what He had done.

In 1922 there was a woman named Mary who was paralyzed from the waist down and extremely sick. Wigglesworth was holding meetings in her town and her friends asked her if they could take her to one of the meetings. Mary agreed but due to her not believing in divine healing, when it came time for her to be prayed for, she did not allow it. The friends brought her home and soon it became clear that Mary was going to die. The friends asked her if she would allow Smith to pray for her if they got him to come to the house. She finally gave in, but by the time Smith arrived, she had already passed. Mary found herself in the throne room of God witnessing light that she had never experienced before. The Lord looked at her and pointed to the doorway that she had just come through, making it clear that He desired for her to go back to earth. As she walked through the door she heard Smith's voice say, "Death, I rebuke you in the name of Jesus." Smith then commanded her to live, and Mary opened her eyes, raised. She was completely healed in addition to being raised, and went on for many years in service to the Lord.

Smith also raised his own wife. Polly regularly said that while she would minister she would get so close to heaven that, "one of these days while I am preaching I'll be off". Like all of us, she longed for heaven and could feel the closeness of heaven at times while here on earth. The heart was made for nearness with God. We were created to walk with Him in the cool of the day, so it comes as no surprise that we long for that Place of eternal light because He is there.

One night, Polly was ministering and suddenly died shortly after the meeting. Smith heard and simply said, "She got what she wanted". He made his way to the funeral and still, being that the Lord commands us to, commanded life into that lifeless corpse even though he knew his wife wanted to stay there. Polly came back for a moment, but the accounts of what happened next vary. Some sources say that Polly said, "Let me go" or "Smith, the Lord wants me." Other accounts say that Smith heard the Lord say, "She is mine and her work is done." Either way, Polly surrendered her spirit that day and Smith did not raise her back again.

Polly wanted to be with the Lord. Everyone understands that and nobody can condemn that desire. At the same time, we have all of eternity to be in heaven; we only have this life to be here. The reality is that we are needed on earth, not heaven. We must remember that we are with the Lord and that we are already seated in heavenly places. When we feel the nearness of heaven and the heavy Presence of God, that shouldn't make us want to die but to take even more time out for prayer. Burnout usually looks like being so overwhelmed with the needs of this life that we want to bail and go to heaven where it would be much easier.

From the start we were made to be near God and to walk with the Lord in the cool of the day on the earth. In other words, the need to be near God is right but how we fulfill that need is where we need wisdom. We were all created with an insatiable desire for God but when hunger for God translates into wanting to leave the earth, we must take some time out from ministry and life, take a sabbatical or vacation, rest, and spend adequate time with God until we feel some portion of satisfaction so that our longing for Him isn't misinterpreted by our hearts into something that subtly kills us. Lovesickness for God is wonderful, but when experienced outside of faith it becomes misapplied and can cause us to miss the whole point of the gift that it is.

You can go to heaven now: Don't buy into believing that you must die to be seated in heavenly places with the King. He died for the very reason to have you seated there the moment you received Him as your savior. It isn't your death that qualifies you to go to heaven; it is His death that has you seated in heavenly places with Him. Through faith you can experience right now what Polly longed for.

William Branham
(1909-1965)

Few walked in the prophetic as accurately as William Branham. Incredible signs and wonders followed his life, including a time when Branham raised a boy from the dead.

In the 1940s Branham received a vision of a child that was hit by a car and killed, then saw himself kneeling down and praying for the boy and him being raised. Branham described the boy's haircut, face, and the color of his eyes. A few different times over the coming meetings when he was preaching Branham would recall this vision and describe it to people.

Years later, Branham was in Finland with Gordan Lindsay and a few other ministers. Near where they were ministering, a car veered off the road and struck a boy that fit the exact description of what Branham had seen in his vision years before. Lindsay and a few others went to the accident and came back crying, overwhelmed by the child's gruesome death. Lindsay told Branham that he should go to the accident and see what had happened, but Branham did not want to go see the child as he was homesick and had a boy about the same age as the child that had been hit; it hit too close to home. After some time, Lindsay finally persuaded Branham to go see what had happened. Branham stood over the body of the boy then turned away, overwhelmed and brokenhearted at what he saw. The moment he turned away though, someone put their hand on his shoulder. He looked, thinking it was Lindsay, but Branham couldn't see anyone there, despite the fact that the hand stayed resting on his shoulder. Branham knew the hand that he felt resting on him must have been an angel, so turned back to the body and asked for the coat that was covering the boy to be lifted up. Every bone was clearly broken in the little body but now Branham's faith was building like Mount Vesuvius. He suddenly declared, "If that boy isn't up on his feet in five minutes, I am a false prophet." They knelt down and began to pray just as he had seen in the vision from years prior. He said, "I pray to thee Lord God, that now you will confirm the word of the Lord that they might know that you're still the Lord, and that Finland would know that you are the resurrection of the dead." Then Branham laid his hands on the child and declared that death had to give this little life up. At that moment the boy stood up and began running around, shouting and praising God. This story was beheld by bystanders and was testified to over the radio and other secular avenues in Finland. Go God.

Oral Roberts
(1918-2009)

Oral Roberts was another man that God raised up during the 1940s healing outpouring, but one of the few that continued on in ministry while others that walked beside him fell on the wayside. God did many mighty things through Oral, and generations to come will benefit from his life.

In 1987, Oral said there were, "...dozens and dozens and dozens documented instances of people who have been raised from the dead" through his ministry. Publicly Roberts only mentioned raising the dead a few times, the previous quote being one of the few, and the backlash from news outlets was significant as a result of these statements. It is clear that raising the dead became something Roberts was not keen to talk about on national television due to the fallout and division that the topic would cause. After learning how divisive the subject was, when dealing with mainstream media Roberts would either refuse to answer how many people had been raised through his ministry or act oblivious to dead raising altogether.

While resurrection has been costly in the past, it is going to become something imperative rather than existing on the fringe. Jesus is the desire of the nations, and He called Himself "The resurrection" (John 11:25). Resurrection isn't a thing, it is a Person. Resurrection is Jesus. In other words, the world is hungering for the demonstration of real compassion and power that is only found in Christ.

Once while Roberts was preaching to a large group of

people a woman began screaming in the crowd. She ran up to the front where Roberts was, yelling that her baby had died. In her arms she held the dead child. Roberts laid hands on the baby and instantly the child was restored.

Though there are apparently many more times Oral raised the dead, it is clear that only those closest to Roberts knew the details of those testimonies. While we must assume that Oral handled the dead raising testimonies he had with wisdom, let us be a people that boldly and joyfully shout from the rooftops the works of the Lord without fear of backlash so that generations to come can feast on the testimonies of the Lord. What God has done, He will do again!

T.L. Osborn
(1923-2013)

T.L. Osborn was an awesome man of God that is known primarily for the crusades they held all over the world. Osborn loved to watch God heal and save, but he also believed in and pursued resurrection power as well. Behind closed doors Osborn told close confidants that God had raised one hundred and twenty people from the dead through their ministry.

One resurrection testimony that Osborn publicly shared was about a dead child that was wrapped up and ready for burial, being carried around aimlessly during a crusade. Daisy, Osborn's wife, called to the mother and told her to come over to her. The mother obeyed and Daisy pulled back the wrappings and saw the dead child. Daisy prayed, the baby came back to life, and the mother began screaming. The screaming was so intense that Daisy asked the mother why she wasn't happy. The mother responded by saying, "My baby had no eyes! No eyes!" Not only had God raised the baby from the dead, but He had also created brand new eyes in the head of that precious child.

David Hogan, a trove of knowledge and experience when dealing with raising the dead, is covered in depth in the next chapter and was deeply influenced by Osborn.

Chapter Nine
(1950-Present)

"It's right to put yourself in a place where if God doesn't come through, you fail."
-David Hogan

David Hogan

Aside from Christ, arguably the most experienced human being in all of history pertaining to raising the dead is David Hogan. David has not only raised many from the dead with his own hands but even more importantly he has taught countless others the ways of faith as well, resulting in their ministry raising more than 500 people from the dead to date. More will be added as time continues.

God sent David and his family as a missionaries to the jungles of Mexico decades ago. The native people were unreached by the Gospel when they arrived, and David began by preaching a simple Gospel backed by healings and miracles. From the start David taught the indigenous indians unwavering faith; they never had to unlearn unbelief like many of us do because they were largely unreached. Their first introduction to Jesus looked like dead raising, crops supernaturally growing, healing, victory over the devil, and intimacy with God. In Mexico persecution, salvations, healings, war, heavenly encounters, resurrections, and confrontations with demonic principalities are common. At times during church services, the Presence of God gets so weighty that they have backup bands ready to take over for when the first batch of worship leaders fall out in the spirit. The second group steps up and takes over the instruments until they can't stand any longer either, then the third.

The miracles that have followed Freedom Ministries come in scores. David has been shot in the head and lived, rode his motorcycle off a massive cliff and sustained no damage, driven his truck underwater without it dying in order to get to a church service, and so much more. Once a man went to rescue an older woman in the midst of a flood and stepped on a massive jungle thorn in the process. Like a nail, the thorn went all the way through his foot. Gangrene set it, and the foot had to be amputated. The man's wife called David and told him that she wanted a new foot for her husband. David came by their home and prayed. A week later he went back and found that the stump now had a bone sticking out of it. Disconcerted, David nonetheless prayed again. A week later David went back to behold an even stranger thing; the man now had a bone foot. No skin, just bones, like a skeleton. Though it was once again disconcerting, David also recognized that it was a creative miracle taking place, so he prayed again. The next week he visited again to find that the man's foot was now covered with skin and completely restored.

David has not only raised the dead, but has died and was raised back by his daughter. When you preach resurrection power it trains those around you to know what to do when the enemy tries to steal, kill, and destroy. The enemy tried to do this to David's grandchild once, taking the child's life. David gathered the family and they began to pray. Every once in awhile David would go over to the lifeless body and touch the child's foot, lifting it up and letting it fall. After some time, the child was restored to life.

While there are countless stories of resurrection that have taken place in Freedom Ministries, two stories in particular stand out. The first took place in a very rural area in the mountains of Mexico. A plague swept through this region and killed the two daughters of a mother. The girls were all this mother had and now they were gone.

Following the laws of the land, she carried her precious daughter's bodies to the designated area, spent the little money she had on a bag of lime, and covered her girl's bodies with the lime. One day had passed. She then hiked for a day over the nearby mountain where she knew some of David's pastors would be. Two days. When she arrived she realized that the pastors were inside and on an extended fast and time of prayer. Instead of interrupting them, she patiently waited outside. This woman had the wisdom not only to seek out the pastor's for help, but to wait. She was wise enough to reason that the most important thing for these men to do is spend time in the Presence of God if they were going to help her. Most desperate mothers would not have the ability to be patient in such a situation, but this woman possessed uncanny wisdom. Three days. When the pastors finally came out of prayer the next morning, the mother related to them what had happened. The pastors, being leaders with servants hearts, hiked back over the massive mountain with the mother to get back to the bodies. It had been four days since the girls died. The two pastors walked up, straddled the lime covered bodies, and called the girls back to life by name. The two sisters both sat up raised from the dead, spit the lime out of their mouths, and were reunited with their mother. Words cannot describe what that mother must have felt.

On another occasion, the two sons of a witchdoctor that had opposed David for decades gave their lives to Jesus. The father was not happy, and cursed his two sons. While a person may be able to get away with witchcraft for a time, at some time you must pay the piper. Anytime a person engages in a transaction with darkness, they seal their own fate rather than determining someone else's by opening the demonic upon their own life. Unless repentance takes place, they must pay because the only system the enemy uses is the law. Thus, the father was soon on his deathbed, suffering from the very thing that he attempted to speak over his sons. His sons, totally healthy, exhorted their father to repent but he would not. The two men then asked Hogan to come. This witchdoctor had been trying to destroy David for many years, so David was hesitant, but he came. When David arrived, the man was very close to death. With his dying breath he cursed his sons, David, and the God that David served. Clearly, this man died in sin. His eternal existence was determined. David and the older brother left, but the younger son suddenly felt a love for his father that he had never felt before. He stayed by his bedside and began to pray for his father's life. He prayed for the whole day and through the night. In the morning his father was raised from the dead. That is incredible, but what is even more breathtaking is that he returned to this life as a follower of Christ.

The son got ahold of David and asked him to come back. David arrived and when he walked into the room, the father fell at his feet, thanking him for bringing the gospel to his people. David was shocked, surprised, and bewildered. The humility that this man was exemplifying was unlike him in every way. David asked the man what changed him. The man told David that when he died he found himself in a dark place. Fear set in, but suddenly he was visited by Christ, full of light. Jesus told the witchdoctor three simple words; "I love you". That was all it took for the man to give his life to Christ. This man went from a witchdoctor to a royal priesthood in three words. Everyone is one encounter away from significant change. The former witchdoctor became a leader in Freedom Ministries and went on to have many more encounters with God, be in leadership, and disciple others.

Most of us have learned that at the moment you die you either go to heaven or hell. This story does not contradict that reality, but gives us reason to see eternal damnation in a more sovereign way. We have been taught that after death, the finality and rigidity of going to either heaven or hell is unalterable. We have been taught that there is no debating or delay; you face judgement once you die and the verdict is irreversible and irrevocable. While this is true we must remember that love never fails. God's arm is strong enough even to reach past the gates of hell and take hold of the prodigals that are His! This befuddles our minds and confounds our theology, but everything we believe must be submitted to a spirit of humility that recognizes that God, in His infinite love and goodness, can do whatever He deems fit to do. He really does desire that none shall perish! His arm is able to save. The moral of the story is that regardless of what state of sin someone dies in, pray that they would be raised from the dead. The younger son's obedience to the love that God gave to him literally saved his father from hell. Did you see that? Resurrection can spare someone from an eternity in hell! Raise the dead.

What has happened and is happening in Mexico is no different than what could happen in first world countries because God is the same God there as He is in America or England. The difference is us. How we were raised in the Gospel dictates how we live it out. The indians in Mexico were brought up in a Christ-centered belief system with a central value of faith. They apply, "Nothing is impossible with God" to every area of their lives; their crops, rain, death, sickness, or anything else. From day one they were taught that God raises the dead. And though we in the Western world want to have faith like that, the only way to do so is by taking up the simplicity of childlike faith again. Again, because we were once that simple. Again, because we were all children at one point in our lives, with no limitations on what reality would look like. Again, because the complexity of our overabundance of learnedness has caused us to lose the faith that is born out of innocent simplicity that we once had. If we believe that resurrections are not common or that there are limits on what God can do, then that reality will manifest. But if we believe, like the gloriously simple indians down in the jungles of Mexico, anything is possible.

David is an undisputed hero, though he would never say that. The way that he ministers to the broken, loves the widow, opposes the proud, and prays for the sick cannot come from anywhere but the love of Christ. I have watched him carry fatally ill children around the room as he weeps over them, watched him cradle my newborn baby boy as he prayed for him, and watched him come undone by God's love during worship. David has eyes that are so lit on fire that they are hard to look into but is also one of the most humorous people I have ever had the honor of being around. The gospel is both serious and incredibly joyful, and David embodies both realities well.

David is a hero because he has put others first in what he does. He has very little regard for himself: He gave his blood for a people group nobody cared about, has risked his own life time and time again for others, and spends his time, energy, and money on others. Such selflessness is most reminiscent of the greatest of Heroes, Christ.

Rolland and Heidi Baker

Rolland and Heidi Baker are missionaries based in Mozambique and quite possibly two of the most wonderful people on the planet. Rolland comes from a family of missionaries that saw incredible miracles in China with young children. Heidi is from Southern California and since 16 years old has had a heart for Christ and loved preaching. They were married and started their ministry many years ago. For quite some time their work as missionaries work could be considered as nothing out of the ordinary, that is, until they began having encounters with God. From that point on, their churches, bible schools, orphanages, and outreaches spread like wildfire.

Almost anything the mind can imagine pertaining to saving human lives and healing those afflicted by the many curve balls life can throw have taken place within Iris Ministries. It is estimated that hundreds have been raised by Heidi and those involved in the move of God they are pioneering in Africa. The deaf hear, the blind see, the dead are raised, food is multiplied, the bullet wounds of those that have been shot miraculously close up and are healed, flood victims are given care, wells are drilled, babies held and brought under roofs that were orphaned, multitudes are brought into the Kingdom, and Jesus is passionately worshipped.

There have been so many reports of the dead being raised in Iris Ministries that it is difficult to tack down an official number, but it is most assuredly in the hundreds. Many of the pastors that have raised the dead refuse to actually tell anyone how many people they have raised;

they do not want the recognition or limelight that comes with raising the dead. Sometimes babies that have died are lovingly held until they are brought back to life, other times the body has been sitting in the African heat for some time and decomposition has already set it. Either way, those praying step out and throw the faith they have at the problem. Surprise Sithole is one of their pastors that has had multiple breakthroughs when it comes to raising the dead. Above all, Iris workers emphasize the love of God and the presence of the Spirit of God. Heidi teaches their people to love the poor as Christ Himself, and the result is that revival is moving mightily in Africa.

Rolland and Heidi will be counted among a precious few in heaven that fully laid their lives down for the Lord, even in the face of martyrdom and extreme sacrifice. If you ever get a chance to see either of the Bakers, do not pass up the opportunity. It is hard to put Heidi's love for Jesus into words. My wife and I adore her. Her hunger for God, her desperation, humility, genuineness, her love for the poor, simplicity and yet learnedness, her brokenness, her boldness, her worship, and her child-like faith leave you without the ability to describe her in a way that does her justice. Rolland may be the most joyful person you have ever seen, despite the incredible tragedies he has witnessed in person.

The Bakers are modern day apostles. They love God and people extremely well. If you want your world turned upside down by Jesus, go to Mozambique and sit at the feet of the poor with them. Your life will never be the same.

Kobus Van Rensburg

Kobus Van Rensburg was a wonderful man of God that was based in South Africa and had a powerful ministry wherein the sick were healed and the dead. Kobus was an excellent teacher, prophet, father, and husband.

Kobus fought cancer all of his life, dying and being raised seven separate times. Kobus strongly believed that Christ actually overcame the spirit of death when he was raised from the dead, and that through Christ, no matter how riddled his body was with cancer, he did not need to die, nor did anyone else that was being attacked by a fatal disease. As confirmation of this truth, not only was Kobus raised from the dead but he raised the dead himself numerous times, sometimes even in his own church services, recorded on tape.

Kobus taught that man was never intended to die from the start, but that it was sin that ushered sickness and death into the world when Adam and Eve ate of the fruit. Kobus strongly believed that Christ was the second Adam, bringing righteousness and removing sin from our lives through His sacrifice. Thus, if the wages of sin is death, then when sin is removed from our lives, death is as well. Kobus embodied this truth every time he raised the dead or was raised.

Once, Kobus was walking up the aisle of his church when he keeled over and died. People nearby saw and began praying for him. Kobus found himself in a field of golden wheat, with the light golden like the sun was just setting. It was beautiful and peaceful. He saw his body laying on the ground and he found himself being pulled away from his body. It was natural, tranquil, and not traumatic. He was experiencing the natural order of things. Suddenly though, Kobus realized that though he was no longer on earth, he still had a will. He firmly said, "No!" in his spirit and instantly, the pull that was moving him away from this body stopped. He began to slowly move back towards his body. He "slipped" back into his body and woke up back in his church. This story reveals to us that just as others have chosen in the past to "go on" and not stay on the earth, we have the power, even when in death, to return. There are many reasons to do so: the ministry, our spouses, our children, our grandchildren, that heaven will always be waiting, that you have one life to spend so spend it thoroughly, and on and on. The reasons to stay are much more substantial and honorable than our reasons for wanting to leave. Let us, like Kobus, embrace the gift of life that Christ so painfully purchased, live life to its fullest, and not accept, invite, or partner with death.

Kobus was a forerunner that the world never fully honored as he deserved. His family has continued on in the ministry, powerfully declaring the truth that Jesus is Lord and Healer.

The DRT

The DRT, or Dead Raising Teams, are groups of people in regions or cities that are prepared at any moment to bring the Kingdom of God to earth. They are modern day minute men and women, but rather than being soldiers like those in the Civil War whose job it was to kill and conquer, this army is ready to manifest the life of God in any situation where sickness and death has taken shape.

Our teams are comprised of normal people that love Jesus. We believe that there isn't a situation where God won't willingly manifest the abundant life that Christ purchased. We believe that Christ commissioned the Church two-thousand years ago to heal the sick and raise the dead in order to demonstrate the reign and Kingdom of God on earth. Over the years, the Church's excuses why *not* to pray for the dead have been abundant rather than their willingness to follow the commissioning Christ already gave us to be releasers of abundant life.

And though we are not opposed to it, we believe it doesn't necessarily take doctorates or studying at universities to become a capable minister of the Gospel. Rather, it is those that have "been with Jesus" that dictates someone being a disciple of Christ. We believe that anyone and everyone that loves Jesus can heal the sick and raise the dead.

People are dying all the time, all over the globe. There is simply too much work to be done on earth to do it any other way apart from everyone being involved and empowered. This empowerment of regular people is the only way that the Church will defeat death to the degree that is being demanded. A leader can be measured by his ability to serve and *empower* those that he is shepherding. If a leader resorts to control to shepherd his people, it is simply an indicator of his lack of faith and overall fundamental insecurity, stemming in fear. And fear, no matter how we try to dress it is up as wisdom, is actually sin. And the atmosphere of sin hinders growth, fruit, faith, and freedom. We must be leaders that shepherd people but empower them, launch them, believe in them, and help them clean up the enviable mess that we all make sooner or later.

And you know what? It is working. At the time of writing, the DRT has had fifteen people raised from the dead. We have over sixty teams in the States and abroad. We have had babies that were dead for longer than a week in the womb raised, the elderly in hospitals, the victim of a massive heart attack, a man that was ran over by a truck, children, a man that had drowned in the ocean, and more.

This is how our teams work. A few people get a vision to have a DRT in their church or city. They invite Tyler out to do a two day event called a School of Resurrection. They gather people that would like to be a part of such a team and have the two day event. After the event, the leaders of the team have a list of contact information of the people that were at the training. When someone dies in their city or region, that list of people are contacted. Some begin to pray wherever they are (work, home, vacation, etc.) and others go to the location of the body and pray in person. The team works with local authorities, honoring what they do, and God gives favor and access as they manifest love in their communities. It is unbelievably simple and beautiful. We have teams that have been given cards by their city or state that give them access into traumatic situations. We have other teams that go out of their way to honor the police and firemen in their city so that they can work alongside them when tragedy strikes. Both the natural and the supernatural aspects of helping people are imperative, and the DRTs honor those in their cities putting their lives on the line for those that are in need.

Our teams function from relationship rather than position, pecking order, or hierarchy. Instead of a pyramid, we function like a web. A pyramid can only cover a small area of ground, but a connected web of Holy Spirit filled believers can cover the globe with ease. Our teams are organic, low maintenance, grassroots, and genuine. Rather than a well oiled machine or organization, they are an organism that grows and moves where it is needed. We are so simple that it actually confounds people with a more traditional idea of what "ministry" should look like. For example, we do not require our teams to have weekly meetings or monthly dues. We actually trust that our teams will continue to follow Jesus even when Tyler isn't there teaching them! We simply stay in contact with our team leads as we would anyone else that we are in relationship with, and are available for whatever they need at any time.

If you want a DRT in your region, church, or city, contact us. We desire for a DRT to be established in every city in the world, not because we want DRTs all over the world, but because the world needs a easily reproducible wineskin that can answer the biggest problem on the earth at this time, or any time; death. Join this army of life.

The Nameless and Faceless

There has been a specific prophesy circulating in the Church for years. It speaks of a great move of God brought about by the "nameless and faceless". I believe that this move of God is currently underway and will continue to build and multiply as we move forward.

This chapter is about you. If you have never had someone tell you that you can raise the dead, this is that. You can. You will. Take it as a prophetic word over your life. I believe in you. I believe in God in you. I believe that regardless how much or how little schooling you have had, you know Jesus and that is all you need. The disciples were unlearned men but *had been with Jesus*. Spend time with Jesus then raise the dead.

Do not let anything disqualify you from what your heart yearns for. In some manner, with some unique facet, you yearn for the rule and reign of God on earth. So what is your part? What are you going to contribute to the overall plan of God on earth? Your destiny is far greater than dying and going to heaven, so what will you accomplish while you are here on earth?
I pray for your dreams to become real to you again. I pray for resurrection life to apprehend the dreams God put in you long ago that you have forgotten about.

You are not small. He who is in you created galaxies that we will never even discover; He is big in you. He is with you, for you, in you, around you, behind you, above you, below you, alongside you, in the future, in your past, and will never leave you. He answers prayers you stopped praying. He loves you as much as He loves Christ, thinks wonderful thoughts of you billions of times per minute, and commands all of heaven to your aid. Even after trillions of centuries in heaven we will never come to the end of new revelations about His goodness. Over and over again new waves of revelation about who He is will wash over us, causing us to fall down again and declare, "Holy, holy, holy is the Lord God almighty, who was, and is, and is to come."

Nothing is impossible for you because God is with you. Whether you are recognized by man or not, do God's bidding. Man may hate you sometimes and may love you other times, but let neither sway you. Love Him and people like you will never have the chance to do it again. Hold your family close. Find a few friends that know your heart and do not spread yourself too thin by giving your heart to everyone. Genuinely love those that mock you and try to ruin your reputation by seeing them through God's eyes. Embrace life on earth and eat of the manna that comes from heaven so you may not die. Live righteous because you want to, not just because you should.

Go for it…raise the dead.

Chapter Ten
(Biblical Accounts)

"Women received back their dead,
raised to life again."
-Hebrews 11:35

Of Oil and Abundance
(1 Kings 17:17-24)

It isn't often that the water that falls from the sky adheres to the commands of men, when to fall and when to be held back, but that is exactly what had been bestowed on him. He didn't know why such power had been given to him, but it was breathtaking nonetheless. And though at first he had treated it like one would dispense cheap parlor tricks, flicking it on and off for entertainment like a three year old does with a light, he had grown now and realized that this had specific purpose. In time he knew it would be used to demonstrate the reality of the God he served, but for now, even his own needs would not be met by using it.

That is how he ended up at the stream. He had been told to go there, and now sat beside the quiet waters, hungry. Having not eaten for a day, he had arrived at the designated stream late the night before, and bedded down on the rocky shore near the water. Late in the night his hunger had awoken him, and instead of going back to sleep he waited for morning's light. Supposedly that is when breakfast would be served.

The sun broke the night's gloom, and light began to stretch across the small riverbed wherein he sat. Distant at first, then louder, he began to hear the calls of ravens. Looking into the sky he spotted them, flying low, a group of a dozen or so. They approached with speed, neared his spot, suddenly extended their wings and swooped to a stop, lightly landing on the ground next to him. Half of the birds carried what seemed to be bundles of leaves in their talons, dropping them only feet away from the Prophet when they landed. The man scooted across the ground and unwrapped the leaves to find that meat and bread were inside.

"Who wrapped this?" the man thought. No rational explanation came to him. He was aware of the obvious answer, but the how still bewildered and intrigued him. Does God Himself prepare meals by hand for His children like a mother in the morning on a school day for her kids?

The man had become somewhat accustomed to miracles. And while the miracles were incredible to behold, they no longer impressed him anymore, at least not as much as what the miracle pointed to did. What the miracles revealed was not first and foremost that God makes the impossible possible, but how involved God was in his life. The miracles were an undeniable sign that pointed to a greater reality; that the Creator Himself wanted to know the Prophet and be known by the Prophet.

For years little questions had popped up in his mind that stemmed from this place of mystery. He no longer asked how it was possible that these impossible things happened, but how it was possible that God Himself was so interested in having a relationship with him when He was God and Elijah was just...Elijah. It took his breath again and again. "Was it He that actually wrapped the food in leaves?" were the kind of questions he asked now, astounded at the thought of God being so involved with what seemed to be small details when there was a universe to be ran. They weren't questions that needed an answer. They were questions that were an answer. They were questions of awe and worship.

He gave thanks and ate.

It went on like this for some time. The birds would come to him in the morning and at dusk. They never faltered. He would eat his fill. He spent his days eating, drinking from the brook, and in prayer. He had nothing else to do. That is, until the stream dried up. It must have happened suddenly, for he had awoke in the morning and found that it was gone. He knew that its disappearance wasn't God's punishment for something he had done; He had learned God didn't work like that. He wasn't offended with God, for he did not believe something as immature as the lie that God was not providing for him anymore. Instead, he knew it was simply time for something else. The stream drying up was an indicator that more was coming, not less.

It wasn't long before he felt the Creator speak to him about what was next. In fact, he had wanted to go to Zarephath for some time, and didn't know why. Thus, the Voice simply confirmed what he already had felt. In addition to where to go, God had also told him that his food would not be given to him from the sky anymore, but from a widow in Zarephath. He knew where to go, and without having the "why" answered, He stood, and began the long walk. There is no asking "Why?" when you truly trust someone. When you are in love the journey is actually more fun when you don't know the "why". Surprises abound.

It wasn't a short walk. He rested at night and walked during the day. Water was the biggest challenge. It was an odd position to be in because God had given him the ability to open and close the heavens by his tongue, but he hadn't heard the Creator tell him to do so, so he did not. He had learned that such power was not to be misused. He had learned that living by what the Voice said to do was the best way to live and because he hadn't heard the Voice tell him to rend the clouds, he didn't.

Finally, after walking for 100 miles, he arrived in the area of Zarephath. He was thirsty (despite finding a spring two days into the walk), and very hungry. He saw the town gates in the distance and made his way towards them, thinking only of filling his stomach and hydrating his body.

As he neared the gates, a woman came into view, dressed in what seemed to be worn clothes, indicating that she was likely poor. She was walking about, near the gate, collecting what looked like sticks.

Elijah was feeling more and more weak by the moment, and though he didn't know if this was the widow that God had spoke of, he called out to her, asking her to get him some water. She looked at him, then seeing that he was in great need she turned to fetch the water. As she left he added, "Some bread as well, please!"

She stopped and turned to face him. "I don't have any bread."

"This must be the widow you had in mind", he thought. He knew it was just like God to send him the broken, the poor, the needy. After all, it is not the rich that need saving.

"I really don't. I only have a small bit of flour and oil, and that needs to feed my son and I. Hence why I am gathering sticks. I am going to use these sticks to make a fire and cook the last of our bread. We have very little. In fact, we have so little that this is our last meal. Unless a miracle happens, we will starve after this pathetic meal. So you can see, I really don't have any bread for you."

Elijah looked at her for a moment. Then he spoke.

"I understand. I'm sure your situation feels terrifying because you love your son. Any mother would feel the same way and would feed her own before a stranger. Here is the thing; miracles do happen. I have seen many miracles. If you take care of me, I will have the ability to take care of you and your son, but if you don't give me drink and food quickly though, I will be of no use to you. I will likely pass out soon from dehydration. Trust me. Trust my God. He will take care of you. I will take care of you. Please."

The woman thought for a moment. She quickly realized that the small meal she was reserving for her and her son would only hold them over for another day, then they would be back on death's doorstep once again from starvation anyways. "It is worth a shot", she thought.

She nodded, then ran through the gate and into the town. Elijah sat down, resting against a nearby wall, exhausted. Some time later the woman appeared again, and fed Elijah the little water and bread that she had. It wasn't much, but it was enough to restore his energy. She helped him up, brought him into the town, and ushered him into her house. The man laid down in a bedroom in the upstairs portion of the house. He needed sleep, and it came quickly.

He didn't know how long he had been asleep, but his waking came suddenly. There was shouting from below, and he rose from the bed and made his way downstairs. The woman and a boy were kneading large portions of dough in the room downstairs, shouting and laughing. Elijah watched as every once and while they would leap away from the table they were kneading the dough on and do a little dance of joy, ecstatically laughing at each other when they would. Elijah found himself laughing as well, which alerted the two to his presence. The widow ran to him and threw her arms around him.

"Thank you. Thank you. Thank you." She said as tears of joy streamed down her face.

"For what?" Elijah said through a chuckle.

"The oil and flour just keeps replenishing. It won't run out. We can make as much bread as we want. In fact, if it keeps up like this, we could feed more than just ourselves; we could feed our neighbors as well!"

The little boy ran up to Elijah and hugged his leg. Seeing the outline of the bones below the surface of the boy's skin and feeling the unpadded embrace against his leg that only comes when bones are wrapped without a healthy layer of fat caused it to dawn on Elijah how close this little family had been to death. This little boy had been starving just a few hours before. He still had a long way to go before he was out of the woods too.

Elijah stayed with them for some time. The oil continued to pour, the flour jar continued to fill. The boy gained weight and the mother was able to sell some of her bread and use the money to buy them new clothes. Neighbors heard of what was happening and of Elijah's God that is a provider, and would regularly stop by for a free meal while hearing Elijah's stories about The Creator.

Then one day it all seemed to go awry. The boy got extremely sick and before they knew it, a few days later he had stopped breathing. The widow's everything was gone. Who cares about oil and flour if her boy was dead? "He can work miracles. Why didn't he heal my boy before he died?", she thought.

It wasn't long before her thoughts became verbalized words. She was thankful for what he had done, but her recent loss brought out a new part of her mother's heart that she didn't know existed. She wasn't bitter per say, but she was not going to settle with her son dying. That was unacceptable.

They were sitting downstairs. The woman was sitting next to the child's body and Elijah was on the other side of the room.

"Why didn't you heal him, Elijah? Did I do something? Are you mad at me?" She asked.

"No dear. Not at all." He replied.

"Then why have you not done anything? If you have the power to give life and you do not do it, you are basically killing him yourself! Do something!"

Elijah looked her in the eyes, tears streaming down his cheeks. Her anger wasn't unrighteous. It was beautiful.

"Give me your son." He said calmly.

She stood, bent over, and scooped up the body. She turned and held him out for Elijah to take. He stood, gently took the body from the mother, and headed upstairs to his room.

"Where are you going?" She asked.

"To pray." He said.

He laid the child down on his bed. It was just two days before that he had been playing with him, both of them wrestling in the dust outside the house. He loved this child. Why had this happened?

"God, did you do this? Are we being punished for something we did?" he said out loud.

He knew better. He knew God wasn't like that. But in times where death has taken its toll, those questions are asked. He was ashamed of himself for thinking of such of thing, but the burning question of "why?" seemed to be overshadowing everything else at the moment.

He took in a deep breath and distanced himself from the situation for a moment. He needed the peace that came when God spoke. He began mentally and emotionally grounding himself on what God had said and done rather than what the circumstances seemed to communicate. He felt his body lose tension, and his mind was no longer swarming with thoughts but was calm. It was then that in the depths of his spirit he heard the words, "The enemy comes to steal, kill, and destroy. I give life and life abundant." It came in a way that he could have missed if he hadn't been listening. It came as a still, small voice. And while it was still and small, it seared itself into his memory like words etched into stone.

"You did not do this, God. You love this child. You are a giver of life." he thought.

Then before he knew it, he was climbing on top of the boy's body. He knew that whatever was of God on his own body needed to rub off on the boy's body. He climbed off, and then back on, three times. It was more of an all-consuming hug than it was simply laying on him. He covered all of the boy each time; sheltering him with life, shielding him from death, hiding him from sickness, and concealing him from what was trying to destroy him.

The third time he was laying on the child, something moved beneath him. It came so suddenly and so gloriously that it gave Elijah a joyful fright and he leap up, staring in bewilderment at the little boy.

Elijah quickly scooped up the boy in an altogether different fashion from the way the mother had downstairs, shouting and laughing hysterically, and ran downstairs with him in his arms. The mother met him halfway through the room, her eyes communicating both disbelief and jubilation.

"Everything you said was true", she said as she took the boy from Elijah and held him close. "Everything you said was true."

A Shunammite's Steadfastness
(2 Kings 4:8-37)

The couple sat sipping tea in the early morning, enjoying the sounds of the awakening city around them; roosters sang at the morning light, children ran down the street readying for the day, and old men walked slowly up and down the streets selling a breakfast of bread and milk from containers they had tied together and slung over their shoulder.

"There is just something about him, isn't there?" The woman said reflectively.

"I fully agree. It's as though, when he is around, everything is peaceful." The man replied.

They sat in quiet for a few moments, until the woman broke the stillness. "You know what people say about him, right?"

The man shook his head.

She lowered her head and voice slightly and said, "They say he is a prophet of the God of Israel."

The man shrugged. "I wouldn't deny it. There is something different about him." An elderly man walked by their open door, looked in, and held up a loaf of bread.

"Tomorrow. We have enough now. " The man sitting at the table replied. The man with the bread nodded and slowly hobbled off.

"I wouldn't mind having him stay with us." The woman said, hinting to her idea.

"I wouldn't either. Having that peace in our house for long periods of time? Sounds good to me."

"I can make up the upstairs bedroom for him then. It isn't like it gets any use anyways, at least not like we had hoped." She said.

Sadly, the man said, "I know. I wish I could give you what you want. What we want. We just got started too late, my love."

Elisha began staying with them on a regular basis. The man and the woman loved his company and honored him with their persistent hospitality. Elisha couldn't help but start to feel the weight of gratitude that the generosity lavished upon him left, so he called his servant to his side.

"Gehazi."

"Yes sir?"

"Go to the Shunammite. Ask her what I can do for her. If she needs favors from high government officials, I can make that happen."

Gehazi did as he was told and returned to Elisha.

"Sir?"

"Yes?"

"Well," stammered Gehazi, "She has always wanted a son. The husband is old and they are unable to have children at this point."

"I understand. Tell the Shunammite to come to me." Elisha said.

Feeling vulnerable that her deepest desire was now known, the woman meekly stood in front of the prophet, waiting for him to speak.

"Sweet woman, around this time next year you will hold your son in your arms." It was not what she expected to hear. She had expected anything but that. It was just too good to be true.

"What do you mean?" She said, less meekly now.

But Elisha didn't respond except with a gentle smile.

"Please sir, do not get my hopes up. Are you sure?"

Elisha nodded, slowly blinking with a shine in his

eyes. Something about the kindness that radiated from him put her heart to peace, and she resolved to believe his words even if it felt like her heart was being lured into a false hope.

Words create. Elisha's were no different. The boy grew stronger every day. The community around them were astounded, with women visiting regularly to hold the boy in wonder at what had taken place, and men slapping the man firmly on the back in congratulations while grinning.

Despite the fact that they were a wealthy family with many material blessings, the boy was their most precious belonging. He was treated like a king in their home, and was a continual reminder to them of the power of the God of Elisha. Their greatest desire had not been too much to ask of this God of Israel. All was well.

Then one day it all fell apart. The boy had gone with his father to oversee the fields. Nobody knows exactly how it happened, but one of the servants came running with the boy in his arms to the father. The boy was screaming as blood cascaded out of his head. He had been hit by some of the reaping tools, and now needed medical attention immediately. The father picked up the boy and ran towards his home. He ran as fast as he could without inflicting more damage on the boy from the jostling. By the time he had gotten home, the boy had lost consciousness. The father left the boy with his mother as he went to get the local doctor.

His mind was spinning with questions: "How did this happen?","Who is responsible?"

But accusations also lashed out from him like knives: "When I find out who did this...", "I thought that God was watching out for us!"

And yet simultaneously, something stemming from a place of self control would bolt in: "There is no time for bitterness and judgements. It will only deter from the now. Focus."

The doctor packed up his things quickly once the father told him what had happened. They sprinted back towards his home, darting down shady alleys and flying past children playing games in the dirt.

They were still a ways off when he heard the unmistakable wail that he knew too well. She had only cried like that once before, and he had hoped then that he would never hear that sound again, as it broke his heart and made him feel a powerlessness that any man abhors.

He knew before he went inside. There the boy's body sat on his mother's lap, arms hanging down limp and the color already leaving his face.

He didn't even make it across the room but crumpled to the floor in absolute agony. He felt the hand of the doctor on his shoulder briefly, then saw the door open and close as he quietly let himself out of their home.

They didn't know what to do with themselves. This is stuff of nightmares. This is the realm of terror, but not terror of what could happen, but what has happened. There is nothing but darkness and loss and hopelessness. Even emptiness is bliss compared to this.

It was hours before they could even part with the body. The women went upstairs and laid the boy down on the bed of the prophet, the same bed from which he had promised her years before that they would have a son.

As he slid out of her arms, she mustered up everything she could to not be embittered towards the prophet. This wasn't his fault, or was it? She had said that she didn't want her hopes dashed, and yet here she was laying her dead son down on a bed, the crimson wound still wet on his head.

Suddenly an anger rose up inside of her. It wasn't the kind of anger she had just been fighting off that stems from bitterness, but an anger that doesn't accept the present situation. They say denial is one of the first stages of grief, but maybe that is exactly how it should be. She realized that she just accepted this whole thing too quickly, as though there wasn't anything they could do about it.

"That is a lie!" She blurted out, without thinking. "If God gave us this child, He can, He will, give us this child again!"

The door slammed upstairs as the woman came leaping down the stairs.

"Sweetie?" The man said in reaction to her speed as he looked up with swollen eyes.

She replied, "I'm going to see Elisha. He will make this right." Her tone wasn't a plea. It was a command.

The journey was around 15 miles. She mounted a donkey with her servant and started on her way. It was going to be a long day, but every minute that passed solidified her growing convictions: This was not okay, and things were not going to stay this way. The immoveable laws that govern this world are bent and even broken by those that are immoveable. It is the violent of heart, the relentless, who bring the Above Kingdom down to earth.

Waves would wash over her, both of rage and brokenness. When the grief would encompass her, something would remind her of her certainty that the situation must change. The grief would lift in that moment of hope mingled with determination.

The prophet saw her first. She was bent over on the

donkey, riding like a dehydrated man that just braved a desert. The waves of heat rising from the sun-bathed dirt distorted her already broken form.

"Go to her." Elisha said to his servant as he pointed in her direction.

Sprinting, Gehazi quickly made his way to the woman.

"Are you ok, dear woman? Is everything ok? What brings you here?"

She was exhausted but looked at Gehazi with eyes full of fire. Her tone was firm. "I want to speak to Elisha I do not have the strength to relate what has happened to anyone else."

"I understand, dear woman. Let me escort you to Elisha."

Gehazi took the reigns of the donkey in his hand and walked in front of the woman and her servant, leading them to the prophet. When they arrived, the woman slid off the donkey and onto the dry, hot ground. She dropped to her knees, surprising Elisha. "What was this woman of wealth doing in the dirt?" He thought to himself. She looked up at Elisha with bloodshot, wet eyes, the dust of the air clinging to the moisture on her face. The moment her eyes locked with his all of her tenacity and anger melted, her gaze fell to the ground, and she began to slowly crawl towards him on all fours.

"My dear woman, what happened?" Elisha asked in a quiet, concerned voice.

She did not respond right away, but grasped Elisha's feet. Elisha bent over and met her face-to-face, gently placing one finger below her chin and pulling her head up so that he could see her eyes.

"Dear woman, what has happened?" He asked again.

She opened her mouth to speak as her tears wetted her cracked lips. "I said not to raise my hopes."

Elisha did not speak, but continued to listen, concern spreading across his face.

In a confused tone she said, "Didn't I say not to raise my hopes? He was my most precious gift from Above."

The prophet stood suddenly. "What do you mean? I haven't heard anything from The Eternal concerning your son. Is he alright?"

"He is...." She couldn't finish the sentence.

"Has he passed to the next world?" Gehazi suddenly asked abruptly.

"Yes." The woman said groaning, drawing the word out like a woman in the depths of birthing pain.

"Hurry Gehazi. Take my staff. Run to the body. Lay my staff on his face."

"Yes sir."

The servant ran so fast that he left a small trail of floating dust in the air, and they watched him as he went.

The woman stood. "Thank you, Elisha. I am so grateful for your care towards me and my family. But until I have that boy back in my arms alive, I cannot leave your side. If I leave your side, I am leaving my child's life back to chance."

Elisha looked at the woman for a moment, then a small smile stretched across his face.

"Of course. How about you and I go to your son?

"Thank you, sir."

They slowly made the long journey. Elisha rode the servant's donkey, and the servant walked alongside the two riders.

It was late into the night when they made out a figure jogging towards them. Gehazi, out of breath, choked out

"I did as you said, Elisha. The boy did not awaken."

The woman, exhausted both emotionally and physically, instantly burst into tears. Elisha rode up beside her donkey and simply placed his hand on her shoulder. She looked at the prophet through newly soaked eyes. All he did was nod.

"He isn't going to give up. I can't either."

She roped herself back together and looked down the road. She was comforted by the lights of Shumen in the distance, signaling the nearing end of the journey. At the same instant she felt the overwhelming pressure and terror of what awaited her in the city; the body of her beloved son.

They arrived at the woman's house sore from the ride. Both tenderly slid off the donkeys to the ground. Walking inside, the man nodded to Elisha and tried to gather up a pseudo smile. Elisha said nothing, but simply grabbed the man's hand as he walked by, making his way to the upstairs bedroom where the body had been laid.

The couple heard the door close to the room as they were going up the stairs to join Elisha, looked at each other, then made their way back downstairs. It seemed as though Elisha wanted to be alone with the body.

Inside the room, Elisha looked down upon the little body of the child he so dearly loved. He had been a part of his life from the very start. In many ways, he felt like the boy's spiritual father, calling him into being prophetically and declaring his existence where he had not yet existed prior.

"Boy, not today." He said, as he crawled upon the bed. He wanted the life that was inside him to get inside this broken body. So he grasped the child's hands with his own and stretched the boy out. He looked the child right in the face and got as close as he could to the boy. He loved the boy, and kissing the child had not been uncommon to him or frowned upon by anyone that witnessed their affection. So he kissed the child. He wasn't even praying so much as he was simply being life. He was loving. He was releasing whatever indescribable thing that caused him to know things others didn't, the thing that caused peace to drape over a home when he was there, the thing that caused him to care for others more than he ever could on his own. Then, without warning, the body started to feel warm against his skin. He got up, walked around the little room conversing with The Eternal, then got back on the child. He didn't care how it looked. The only One that was watching was God Himself.

He didn't recall how long he was there before it happened. A sneeze was not what he was expecting, but that is what the child did seven times. Then the boy opened his eyes. The wound on his eye had closed, and blood was no longer coming forth from it as it had before.

"Gehazi!" Elisha shouted downstairs.

The servant came running up the stairs. "Yes sir?"

"Get the Shunammite."

The woman came slowly up the stairs. Elisha watched her from the top of the stairs, the door closed to the room. She looked both fearful and hopeful. Hopeful for obvious reasons, and fearful for opposite obvious reasons.

"Take your son." Elisha said as he opened the door to his bedroom.

Because his statement didn't tell her of the outcome, good or bad, she did not react until she got into the room and saw for herself.

There are few embraces like the one the followed. The

husband came running upstairs shortly after because of the joyful noises that were coming from the above room, and soon the small family was in one embrace, the parents essentially hugging each other with the boy stuck between.

The peace that had initially rested over their home when the prophet came returned to them, and the life that they had initially asked God for had as well.

Elisha smiled, closed the door to his bedroom so that the newly rejoined family could have time alone, walked downstairs, then out the front door. He would be back another day but for now, his much needed work here was done.

A Deceased Resurrection
(2 Kings 13:21)

The disease came on quickly, to his surprise. Despite the miracles, despite the anointing, despite the heavenly interventions that so frequently cascaded into his life. It must be noted that even men of God get sick. Unlike his spiritual father, Elisha's disease eventually led to death. The body was buried in a tomb, not far from where a woman named Huldah lived.

Like Elisha, Huldah had not seen Shallum's death coming, despite her prophetic insights. Nonetheless, one evening she stood over her husband's body weeping, wondering how she would go on without him. She felt alone, abandoned, and powerless. The worst feeling in the world is not depression, loss, pain, or insanity, for those things can be remedied. Powerlessness is the reality of incapability to change the things life throws at us, thus it is the pinnacle of human terror.

Some of the Israelites came and gathered up the body in a white cloth, wrapping it with the gentleness that one uses when holding a new born child. Huldah watched from the front door of her home as the men disappeared from sight on their way to the graveyard where they would lay the body of her beloved. Forever. "He won't come back home in a few days. He is gone." The thought slowly settled into her mind. It was then that Huldah was ambushed by the thought of how permanent death felt. The thought of burial didn't come as a relief to her as it seemed that it did to others. To many it was laying their loved ones to rest, a peaceful goodbye and sending off to tranquility, but to her it felt like a whole new level of finality. There was no going backwards to yesterday. If she could just have had yesterday to live over again maybe they could have gotten him better medical attention. Now there would be no more sitting on the front porch in the cool of the evening together. No more anniversaries. No more romance, laughter, silly morning wrestling, or the sacrificial joy that comes from getting outside yourself and actually understanding another person's point of view.

And it wasn't just Shallum being buried six feet under was all that she was losing. His death had also been the nail in the coffin to her own faith slipping away. She didn't want it like that, but she didn't have the energy to fight to stop it from happening either. Her faith was being sealed away below the ground with her husband, and that scared her as much as being alone did. She wanted to believe, but she felt as though she had no control over the torrent of emotion that her heart floated upon. That river of pain did not feel like it led towards the God of her forefathers, but more likely, away from Him. She was conscious of her diluted feelings towards her Creator since the moment that she discovered her husband's lifeless body laid out on their living room floor. Cold. Breathless. Colorless. Some part of her heart died when Shallum did.

The men laid the wrapped body down on the ground, then began to use shovels and pickaxes to break up the ground and dig a hole. Even with all of them working it was going to be a few hours before they got the hole big enough to lay the body in it, due to the hard, dry earth they were attempting to burrow through.

One of the men suddenly froze. The others looked up, sweat dripping off of their faces, locking their eyes on the man that went still.

"What is it?" One man asked in a whispered voice.

"I thought I heard something." The still man said.

The others, all color now drained from their faces, slowly lowered their tools and listened as well. It was no false alarm. The others heard the noise as well, and it sounded like what they were all on guard about: Moabite raiders. Each of them had heard the stories of what happened to people who got between a raider and their buried spoil in the graveyards. The Moabites likely brought weapons, while the Israelites only had their tools.

"We must go! Quickly!" Said the man that first heard the noise. He knew that they couldn't leave Shallum's body laying out in the sun, so he quickly scanned the graveyard for a place to put the body until they could sneak back in and give it a proper burial. He saw the opening to the tomb of Elisha, and though it was not ideal, it was their only option.

"Come! We must put him in there!" He said.

"In Elisha's tomb? Are you sure?" Said another man.

"We have no choice!" Said the first man in a rushed and forceful whisper.

A few of them gathered up the tools while a few men grabbed the white cloth wrapped around the body. With one quick motion they heaved the body through the air and into the tomb. They then turned to quickly run out of the graveyard and away from the Moabite raiders.

At first they thought they had it made. The sounds they heard behind them and didn't seem to be paying any attention to them. Each man seemed to relax a bit, their shoulders dropping and composure exemplifying less tension than back when they were digging the grave.

There were a few large boulders to make their way

around, then they would be completely in the clear. It was then that a man stepped out from behind the boulder, walking out onto the path that the Israelites were on. He simply smiled, a large dagger in one hand, the other hand playing with the razor's edge of the blade. A shield was slung over his back, and his upper garments revealed his large, uncovered biceps. He was a tall man, sculpted for war. As soon as he stepped out, countless men stepped out from the boulder as well. The last to come forth from behind the large rock gave a little whistle, and suddenly all of the men that were behind them in the graveyard were now at the Israelite's rear. They were surrounded.

The large man spoke, "This is how this is going to go. You are going to lay down your pathetic tools so that none of you do anything you regret. You are also going to strip. We want your clothes and anything else you have. If you refuse, then you die. And that means a long day for my men and I digging holes to put your pathetic corpses in, so please don't make this harder than it needs to be."

He turned to his men and thundered, "Where is my armor bearer? I don't want to carry this sword and shield any longer! That little runt of a man that is always trailing behind."

One of the Moabites behind the small group of Israelites hollered out, "He was in the graveyard with us last I saw him."

The large man shook his head. "He will probably show up panting in a few minutes, like he always does!" The raiders bellowed in cruel laughter.

"Nevermind that! Back to the matter at hand. Strip!" He commanded of the Israelites.

The man that first heard the Moabites, the leader of the little group of Israelites spoke, "Sir, if we do as you say, do I have your word that you will not harm my men?"

The large man roared in laughter. "Of course!"

The Israelite leader did not believe the bear-sized man, but he had no choice. "Men, you heard him. Today we lose our dignity but not our lives."

Just as the Israelites were about to disrobe, a small, lanky man walked up behind the Moabites in the back.

"Sir! The runt is here!" Yelled one of the raiders.

"Get up here!" The large man said.

The lanky man walked up to the front. Following him was another man. Due to the weapons pointed at them and the inevitable stripping they were all preparing for, the Israelites weren't paying much attention to the lanky man and his companion.

"Sir," said the lanky man, "you need to hear what just happened."

The large man glared at the lanky man. "I do?"

"Yes. I was in the graveyard just now, when I heard the whistle. I began walking up here to meet up with you. I happened to walk by Elisha's grave."

"Wasn't he that man of Israel that was considered to be a prophet?" Asked the strong man.

The crowd of Moabites murmured in the affirmative.

"What of it? What happened?" Growled the big man, feeling as though his time was being wasted.

"Well...he is what happened." The lanky man pointed to the man that had followed him up to the front.

The man stepped in front of the lanky man to face the leader of the raiders. It was only then that the Israelites realized who he was. They gasped.

It was Shallum.

"What is this about?" The leader yelled, not

understanding what had happened or why the Israelites were gaping at the man standing in front of him.

"He...was dead." Said the leader of the Israelites.

"Rubbish. Now strip!" Said the raiding leader.

"It is true." the lanky Moabite asserted frankly. "As I walked by the tomb of Elisha, I happened to glance inside. The body of this man was wrapped and slowly rolling into the tomb. These men must have thrown the body in when they heard us raiding the tombs. I watched and the moment this man's body rolled far enough into the tomb, it was like lightening hit the place. He leapt up and stood on his feet, despite the wrappings!"

The lanky man was now shaking as he spoke, but he continued on.

"Then he tore the wrappings off of himself and walked out of the tomb like nothing happened! I am telling you, this is the witchcraft of the God of Elisha...the God of Israel! Do nothing to these men sir, I beg you! We would be calling curses down upon ourselves to harm them!"

The large man now stood quiet, a little color drained from his face. His eyes darted between the dead man that was now alive and the lanky man. Something like fear slowly overshadowed him, not unlike the way a cloud casts its darkness on earth by briefly covering the sun on a bright day. The intimidating composure that had been the man's trademark suddenly melted into a form of meekness that is typical of an elderly man that is at the end of his life.

His words were softer now, "I have heard of magic like this. It is not to be trifled with. Keep your clothes on, you dogs. While you don't deserve to walk out of here with your lives let alone your meager belongings, your

God has saved you from my hand. Speak to Him on my behalf."

The leader of the Israelites spoke more boldly now, "Because of your wisdom to not harm us this day, we will pray to Him that He will have mercy on you and draw you into His everlasting love."

The strong man nodded. At one wave of his hand, the raiders turned and began to walk away in unison with the little band of Israelites looking on, watching them leave.

The silence was broke by Shallum. "I must find my wife. I am sure she is overcome with worry and grief. I need go to her at once."

The Israelites watched as Shallum sprinted out of the graveyard, each bewildered by this running man that was clearly dead only minutes prior.

Shallum walked up the door of his house, wondering what would be the best way to reveal himself to his wife. He knew that such an occurrence would cause her a lot of shock, but he couldn't think of any gentle way to do it, so he simply knocked on the door.

He heard footsteps inside, then the familiar creak of the door as it swung open.

She simply stared at him for a few moments. He wondered for a brief moment if she was going to close the door again, telling herself that she was just imagining things, but she suddenly flung herself into his arms unreservedly. She was not crying, but uncontrollably weeping in relief and joy. He stood there holding her as neighbors and those passing by stopped, drawn to the spot by the sounds of her wailing, silently beholding the impossibility that was now not just possible, but reality.

Shallum spoke quietly in her ear as they embraced. "I saw our Creator. He told me to tell you that there is no situation where you are powerless. We are not powerless because God is not powerless. He is for us, who can be against us?"

At the sound of his words she only wept harder, with more joy.

The Widow's Son
(Luke 7:13-15)

Aliza wanted to die. This felt like the final blow to the minuscule amount of will she had to have in order to continue on, and as the crowd walked beside her on the way to the graveyard to bury her son, she couldn't help but think of how easy it would be to intentionally allow her life to slip away from her. She thought of a nearby river and how easy it would be to jump in and not come back up.

"Who would miss an old widow anyways?" she thought to herself. "At least then I would be reunited with both of them."

Despite how disturbing her thoughts may feel to someone who hadn't been through what she had, to her they simply felt like reasonable logic. In her eyes, there simply didn't seem to be much of a reason to stay alive anymore.

It wasn't just that Chaim had died. While the death of a son would irrevocably crush most people, and it definitely contributed to the downward spiral she now found herself, it alone hadn't been her doing in. The pit she found herself in was deeper than one loss. Not long before Chaim's death, she had also lost the love of her life. Her husband's death started the seemingly unstoppable train of momentum of loss and destruction in her life, but at that point she hadn't yet lost the will to live. After all, she had a son to care for. He gave her a reason to live. She watched him choose to be strong as he had to do what no son should ever have to do; bury his own father. She had been so proud of him for the way he had chose to continue on and not give up on life. During that time the two of them grew incredibly close because of the loss and pain they both experienced and had to work through. All they had was one another. They had to relearn how to do life; how to manage conflict, how to lead, how to bring in an income, how to fix all the things around the house that broke so regularly, how to hold each other when they needed strength and empathy, and on and on. Everything that dad had done, they had to pioneer in their own lives and embrace. They had grown so close. Aliza would have never guessed that one day she would also lose the one other person she had in the whole world. Chaim was all she had left. Now she had nothing.

"What is the point to anything now?" she thought to herself as tears ran down her face. Every step towards the graveyard was arduous, like her feet were made of lead instead of flesh. She reasoned to herself that lead would work better for the river anyways. It was at that moment that she decided that that day was the first and last day she would live alone. Tonight she would dine with her family again. The choice to take her own life gave her a fleeting sense of power, as there was finally was something she had that couldn't be taken from her. Nobody could blame her; she was tired. She was tired from loss. She was tired from having to overwork herself to make ends meet because of the void that her husband left financially. But most of all, she was tired of being alone. Loss had worked her to the bone like a harsh taskmaster, and all she wanted was to be free of its merciless grip.

The crowd of mourners made their way around a bend in the road before exiting through the town gate. As they exited, another crowd met them that was going in.

Aliza couldn't help but notice the drastic difference of mood between the two crowds. Her's, understandably, was of grief and sadness. Their's was of joy and excitement. Something about the contrast shook Aliza out of her stupor.

As the crowds began to mingle together like rivers flowing in opposite directions, Aliza saw a man walking towards her with a child on his shoulders. Everyone seemed to be clinging to him, and it was clear that He was the reason the joyful crowd was gathered.

Something about this man captivated Aliza, and she found herself gazing at him. The man got closer and closer, when suddenly the smile that He had on his face disappeared and was replaced with a serious look as he scanned the crowd with his eyes. After a moment his eyes found hers, and his searching ceased. They stood but a few feet from one another, with locked eyes. Jesus surveyed her situation, looking to the right to see the coffin upon the shoulders of the friends of Chaim, and back to the tears that filled Aliza's eyes.

"Don't cry." He said quietly.

His words felt like the first breath of air her suffocating heart had breathed in days. Such a statement would likely have been offensive coming from someone else, but the way He said those two words was with so much gentleness and love that it could have never offended her. His words possessed so much heartbreak, pain, empathy, and compassion. The way He said those two words made her wonder if He had known Chaim, because only someone that had known her son could have uttered such a simple statement with so much care. Only someone that has experienced equal if not greater pain than what she felt could empathize as much as He had with just two words. She felt hope and didn't know why. Something had splashed over her dry soul. It was as though she knew that this Man only said not to cry because He was about to give her a reason not to cry. Involuntarily, she held her breath, wondering what this Man would do next.

He smiled at her, then walked a few feet over to the coffin and touched it with His hand. Then He joyfully called out in a loud voice, "Young man, I say to you, get up!"

There was a moment of silence, and the Man kept His hand on the coffin. Then surprisingly, just as Aliza's hope was about to flee, Chaim sat up. To everyone's shock, he looked at his mother and started speaking quickly to her, telling her how it is okay and that father is well, of things in heaven, and on and on. Aliza stared at her son for a few moments, then suddenly ran to the Man and threw herself into His arms. He did not recoil, but held her tight, then gently kissed her on the head like a father does to a daughter. There was a moment of complete depth and understanding as their eyes met, then He suddenly broke out in loud laughter as swept her up in His arms, gently lifted her off the ground, and swung her side to side.

The two crowds had now become one and started cheering His name in unison. Soon dancing broke out, and the gate to the town was unusable to anyone that was trying to enter or exit for quite some time. Chaim was brought to the ground and ran over to his mother, who was clinging to Jesus' arm. He hugged her tighter than he ever had before, then released her and grabbed Jesus' other arm. The three of them danced together, Jesus in the middle, spinning them wildly about.

"He restores the family!" the crowd declared.

"He redeems the grave!" they shouted.

As Aliza danced, she prayed quietly, "I want to live again. Thank you for my son. Thank you for your love."

Jairus' Relief
(Matthew 9:25)

The only temporary escape they had was by boat. It was then, gliding across those blue waters, that the masses didn't desperately push up against them to the point of crushing them.

It was not as though it bothered Him though. He knew their needs and why they came so adamantly to Him. They were a people without a shepherd, despite the many synagogues and religious leaders that were available.

Jesus stepped out of the boat first, a large smile on His face, and many children on the beach ran to Him. The children clambered all over Him, a few even clinging to His legs so that He couldn't walk without lifting each leg, now heavy because of the added weight of the laughing children. Jesus didn't seem to mind, and all of His attention was on these little ones despite the large, impending crowd that gathered around Him. Some shouted requests to Him from the back of the crowd, others interjected their thoughts and needs from the front. Due to their comments it was clear that some simply wanted His approval. Others wanted healing for themselves or someone they loved. Still others just wanted to talk with Him, as though they had never had a friend they could truly trust. Amazingly, Jesus kept a gentle, joyful composure through it all. The disciples watched from the boat for a moment before disembarking, most of them in awe of not just the fact that He could do miracles unlike anyone else, but the way He handled Himself with the public. Everyone was so needy and overwhelming, yet Christ always was patient with them. The people simply hadn't encountered tangible love like this amidst the temple or synagogues rulers.

A leader of one such synagogue approached the large mass surrounding Jesus. He was wearing a long robe, extravagant in color and quality. He looked haggard and worn out despite the clothes he donned, and the cause had been a long morning and afternoon facing the apex of most men's nightmares. You would think that dealing with a close-to-death daughter would be enough, but he also had to defend his desire to come see Jesus to his many friends and co-leaders. They had all offered their prayers on his daughter's behalf, but it had done nothing. When Jairus had announced to them that he was entertaining the mere idea of going to a man that he had heard so much about and asking him to pray for his daughter, he had thought that he would have their support. He thought that they were as desperate as he was but he had been wrong. He had come to a place where he didn't care where the miracle came from, as long as it took place. Desperation had tore down his pride and his fastidious tastes when it came to who he received spiritual insight from. His fellow leaders did not feel the same way. It was as though they were more at peace with his daughter dying than taking a risk and going to a controversial source for help. First they started with warnings about deception and getting demonized by the man's touch, but when he made up his mind to go, they did not warn any longer. They simply told him that he was deceived and probably already filled with demons. It wasn't long before a meeting had taken place without Jairus' knowledge, and he was quietly informed that it had been decided by his peers that he no longer held the position of synagogue ruler. On a morning where all he needed was support and encouragement he had found nothing but abandonment and criticism from those that he had not only considered to be his fellow ministers, but his friends.

And while it hurt, he also understood why it happened. Not long ago he would have never dreamed to listen to woodworker from Nazareth about spiritual issues, so the position of his previous friends wasn't foreign to him. But now that his daughter lay on the doorstep of death, he didn't care where the person hailed from or what profession they were in. If this man could save his daughter, woodworker or not, it seemed like common sense to go to him. Tragedy has a way of stripping down everything you think you believe and revealing what is of actual importance, causing you to drink unfamiliar sources you previously deemed harmful.

Oddly enough, when he was given word of the decision that was made about his position in the synagogue, an incredible amount of hope rose up in him that he did not expect. It wasn't because he wanted to be free of his role in the synagogue, for he loved the work he did before God. Hope rose in his heart because he knew that there must be something about this man if all of his friends, whom he had always known were strung a bit tight, were so adamantly opposed to him when all Jesus had done was heal people and drive out demons.

The leaders had moved the body from the synagogue to his home due to his decision, and it had felt like their way of washing their hands of the situation and leaving Jairus and his daughter to their own demise. They spoke of "handing them over to satan", and offered a few prayers asking that God would be merciful to them for their decisions. It was then that Jairus left his home to go to Jesus.

Nobody in the crowd knew the kind of desperation that Jairus had stored up in his heart. He realized that this wasn't the synagogue; there were no neatly formed lines and quiet prayers. He knew there was nobody there that needed a miracle more than he did, and thus he wasn't gentle in his attempt to get near Jesus. This was the moment to receive what his daughter needed, and if he had to push to get what he needed, then he would push hard, for this moment may never present itself again. There is a place in prayer where you are not "thoughtful" towards those around you; You are there solely to get what you need.

Jairus fell at Christ's feet and as words started flowing out of his mouth tears did the same from his eyes. He had rehearsed over and over what he was going to say, but when the moment came it all went out the window. There was only enough time to say what he needed. He needed his daughter to be well or she would die.

Jesus immediately pulled Jairus to his feet and listened carefully to him. Jairus quickly explained the situation and at the end Jesus simply nodded to him. Jairus grabbed Jesus' hand and led him out of the crowd. He held Jesus' hand tight as he fought against the waves of people, and felt Jesus squeeze his hand back. He looked back at Jesus when this happened, and Jesus gave him a gentle smile. It was at that second that Jairus knew that his daughter would be healed.

The crowd continued to follow Jesus and press against them despite their moving forward. Suddenly, Jesus said in a loud voice, "Who touched my clothes?"

Everyone looked at one another in confusion, for everyone was touching Him. Nonetheless, Jesus kept looking around to see who had touched Him. A few moments later a woman fell at his feet and while trembling with fear, confessed that she been the one that had touched Him and been healed of non-stop bleeding that had caused her to go into poverty due to the doctor bills. People went quiet as she spoke, for what she had done was not socially acceptable because she was considered by all to be unclean. Something in Jairus resonated with the woman. Both of them had been cast aside. Both of them had risked everything to get near Jesus. Jairus watched Jesus' response to the woman carefully, as it would show him how in-tune this man was to people's motives rather than what was the moral status-quo.

"Daughter, your faith has healed you. Go in peace and be freed from your sufferings." The woman stopped shaking and lifted her eyes to Jesus in a bright smile. He smiled back at her, then took her hands and lifted her to her feet. He had no condemnation or condescension in His voice as He spoke to the woman. He seemed proud of the woman for doing that which was considered socially inappropriate rather than disappointed in her. It was exactly what Jairus hoped for.

As the crowd rejoiced over the miracle the woman's healing, a few men from Jairus' house showed up.

The Weeping God
(John 11:43-44)

Lazarus was sick for some time. They had sent word to Jesus, but He had not shown up. And just like they feared, early one morning Lazarus slipped away.

Mary had done her best to not be offended with Jesus. She knew He had the power to make her brother well, but for whatever reason, He had not. That fact caused questions to run through her mind and heart like a flooded riverbed when a dam breaks upstream.

"Why didn't He come?"

"Doesn't He remember the oil?"

"Has He forgotten that we love Him?"

Her heart attempted at answers. She tried to give Jesus the benefit of the doubt, but again and again her attempts to defend His lack of action was overshadowed by the stark reality that Lazarus was gone. Thus, try as she might to quiet them, the bombardment of very reasonable questions continued to rain down upon her.

After her brother died, every moment that passed was torturous. The minutes turned into hours. Hours turned into days, and each day felt like a month. She would try to fill her thoughts with something aside from Lazarus' departure, but death has a way of being the slap that brings those that have lost a loved one back to the reality that the person is altogether gone. Soon all Mary wanted was an escape from the constant pain. She found that sleep was the only thing that kept the agony momentarily at bay, and discovered that there is a blissful moment after waking but before total consciousness where she would be without recollection of what had happened. Unfortunately, those moments were fleeting as grief would suddenly sweep over her afresh and remind her of the irrevocable situation she was in. When this would happen it was like rediscovering that Lazarus had died all over again, thus every morning was the dawn of a new nightmare. Mary found herself in a nightmare not when she slept, but when she woke.

People said that it would get better over time. Mary wanted to believe them. She knew that they meant that the sting of death dulls some as time goes on, but she also knew that essentially, things really wouldn't get better unless her brother was at her side again. She instinctively knew that the answer wasn't to let time heal her wounds; the answer was to get her brother back.

This thinking started to creep up in her heart. This hope synonymously scared her and encouraged her. On the one hand, this sprouting desire scared her because she wondered if she was setting herself up for an even bigger disappointment, but on the other hand she had nowhere else to turn. Mary had heard about the son of the widow from Nain that Jesus had brought back to life. Jesus obviously possessed supernatural life; where else did she have to go? She had no real, concrete answer to her torment other than receiving her brother back to life. As she started to remember who Jesus had been to her, this hope transformed into more of a knowing. She didn't know how to explain it, but she was sure that if she could look Jesus in the eye and tell Him that her heart was broken He would not allow her heart to stay that way. He had always been such a safe place for her. He had never done anything that alluded to Him being okay with leaving her in a place of pain or loss.

Then one day while Mary was resting in her room, Martha came and told her that Jesus was nearby and asking for her. Lazarus had been in the tomb for four days, and deceased even longer. Something leap in her heart when Martha said that Jesus was asking for her, and as she walked to the place where He was, she found herself imagining what it would be like to see

Lazarus come forth from that dank, dark tomb they had left his body in.

Then, there He was. Even from a distance she met eyes with Him. He did not look away in shame, but beamed at her. She found herself running towards Him, images of her brother alive and well flashing through her head, and she crumpled at His feet.

"If you had been here, my brother would not have died." Mary declared. Her words were more of a declaration of His love and power towards her and her brother than a statement of offense that Jesus hadn't raised Lazarus. Mary knew that Jesus could, and more importantly would, raise the dead.

Then Mary began to weep uncontrollably. She wept for many reasons; the pain, the questions, the loss, the confusion, but also because of hope. She so desperately wanted those images that crossed her mind of her brother alive and well to be true. Tears streamed down her face, and when she saw that Jesus was also weeping, she cried all the harder.

It was then that Jesus' love dawned upon Mary in a new way. He wasn't distant from her pain, even though He had the power to change her situation. Though He had the ability to raise Lazarus from the dead, He seemed to be in no rush to move on from the feelings she was presently experiencing. Before He did anything else, He was determined to partake of and relate to the heaviness that Mary was experiencing, so that for one moment she may feel loved again in the midst of this terrible situation. His tears substantiated her questions and validated how she felt. His tears showed that He understood. His weeping revealed that He didn't reprimand her for the times when she was offended with Him. His tears showed her that He sits with those in pain, weeps with those that weep, and is the most compassionate, wonderful Being in all of the universe.

She walked with Him to the tomb, leading Him by the hand.

They both could not stop crying. Jesus always carried Himself like someone of royalty, but He now walked with heavy feet and a slouched posture that communicated brokenness, like Mary. Soon they looked up and saw the cave wherein Lazarus' body was.

"Take away the stone." Jesus said.

Due to being caught up in raw emotion with Jesus, Mary hadn't noticed anyone else with them so Martha's voice came to her as a surprise.

"But Lord…"

Mary saw Jesus turn to Martha and speak to her, then He turned back, wiped the tears from His eyes, and then He began to pray.

She knew it was about to happen, even though it hadn't yet. Somewhere unseen there was something of power building, about to be released. When Jesus told Lazarus to come out of the tomb, Mary knew He would.

And he did. Lazarus came forth from his tomb, wrapped in linen. The mourners that had followed them to the tomb went silent. Mary and Martha ran forward, tearing the strips of cloth off of his face and hands. Some rejoiced, while some that stood by did not. From that day on, the chief priests and Pharisees plotted to take Jesus' life.

Jesus ran forward and held the family of three in His arms. His tears were gone, as were Mary's. Martha was bewildered. Lazarus simply smiled at Jesus and said,

"I knew You would come through."

Jesus smiled back.

Many Raised
(Matthew 27:52-53)

The centurion had the task of guarding the heretic as He hung along with a few others. He stood below the man hanging on the cross, head tilted upwards, watching His broken body fight for every breath. The breathing slowed, the man bellowed a few words, then went limp. Aside from few nearby women breaking into loud wailing, a strange silence enveloped the place. Everything went quiet, but in a way that didn't necessarily have to do with sound; it was a curious stillness like even the greek gods of old had gasped. It was as though even the invisible had taken notice.

It was clear that this self-proclaimed king was finally dead, and at that moment, to his surprise, many things took place that astounded the soldier.

First, the ground shook violently as though the earth itself was rolling over in its grave. The soldier fell down due to the shaking, and from his hands and knees he looked up and watched the buildings and trees nearby sway and vibrate. The timing was just too coincidental to be a coincidence, and memories suddenly began to assail his mind, reliving them from a different perspective. He remembered earlier the day flogging the man, watching in slow motion as the whip rose and fell, flicking spatters of blood on the ground and nearby wall. Unexpectedly, he noticed the man's eyes. They were oddly kind and looking right at him, into him, through him. The memory changed. Flashing through his mind he saw the crude hammer as he slowly lifted it into the air, moments from driving the massive nail through the man's wrist and again, there were those eyes. Eyes that were not angry. Eyes that lack condemnation, blame, or even the slightest tinge of resentment. "How can that be?" He thought to himself.

The memories ceased as his eyes fell upon a nearby hillside where a cemetery was located. The rock wall that was the home to many tombs of those that had died was trembling with everything else. The wall formed by the hillside split in numerous places like a window does when struck by a rock. Large cracks appeared across the face of the wall, branching out like a spiderweb.

What followed was beyond all comprehension and logic. The soldier watched bewildered as people began to crawl and walk out from the tombs that had been broken open. The earth's shaking stopped. The centurion clambered to his feet, his eyes glued on the graveyard. It wasn't just a few that were coming forth from their graves, but many. Those that were coming forth no longer had the slightest appearance of death about them, and He lost count as to how many there were. They seemed to be completely fine, as though they had never been locked away in the tomb to begin with. He blinked stupidly a few times, hoping that when he did he would come to his senses and see a normal setting. After all, eye problems would be easier to understand than what he was beholding. Part of him had wondered if the long day had caused him to fall asleep and now he was in the land of dreams. Yet when he spun around, he found that the man just as they had left him, still hanging on the cross, crimson puddles still gathering below him. He looked back to the cemetery in disbelief. The number of people had increased even more. He squinted, trying to make out what they were doing after being liberated from their stone prisons by the earth, but it seemed that they were walking about, greeting each other.

Skepticism gave its last hurrah in his mind. Was it a well planned ploy planned by the followers of this hanging man so that the Romans would somehow be intimidated and take him off the cross? If so, how did they make the ground shake? The centurion quickly concluded that no man could have orchestrated such an event. This was no cheap parlor trick, but real magic. This was the stuff of legends. Thus, he reasoned that if the quake was real, then the resurrections had to have been real as well, which only left one conclusion about this self-proclaimed messiah on the cross.

"Surely He was the Son of God." The centurion said out loud. The Father smiled.

A few days later the centurion heard the news that Jesus had come forth from His grave and was alive. Many did not believe it, but he did. He had seen what the God of Jesus did in the graveyard just days before, and it was greater than anything the greek gods had ever done. "Of course Jesus was raised" he said to himself. "If God could raise many people from the dead in the graveyard, how much more His own Son?"

The centurion found out that after Christ was raised, the people he had witnessed be raised from the dead in the graveyard went into the city and appeared to many people. He had not told anyone about what he had seen, so the fact that others reported that the people existed and had in fact been raised came as a comfort to him. He had wondered if he had imagined it all or worse, if he was losing his sanity.

From that day forward, when someone mentioned Jesus to him, the centurion would repeat what he said the day he witnessed the event in the graveyard, "Surely He was the Son of God."

Securing Abundant Life
(Matthew 27-28)

The vinegar was still wet on His lips. His eyes searched and found her, hand over her mouth in shock, yet an acceptance in her eyes like she had known all her life that this day would inevitably come. She was both in the trauma of unexpected pain and yet expected it all along. He had told her and He was never wrong, that she had learned. He looked at her, trying to speak as best as He could with His eyes, putting her heart to rest, but she looked away as the tears overtook her once again. It had been a very long day, and she couldn't take in that last moment that she knew was coming. More than the pain in His own body, it was watching those He loved watch Him that broke His heart the most.

And though there was no moment in all of the history of humanity when a person was more abandoned and deserved it less, there was nonetheless a stillness that was undeniable. One had not left Him. His heart smiled though His body could not, and He secretly reveled in the nearness. Through cracked lips the cry of David crept from His mouth because while it felt like He was abandoned, He knew He was not. He knew it was impossible for The Eternal to hide His Face from Him. He was always there; the undeniable truth regardless of how things felt or how bad circumstances got.

He knew they couldn't kill Him. It was impossible. They couldn't take His life; He had to lay it down. He had to let go in order for it to go according to the plans written long ago. He had decided it before the core of the earth had been heated white hot, and in many ways one could say that He was already dead. It could be argued that He always had been, but only so that life could become even more abundant and verdant. For life without death is not really life, and it is only when a seed dies that it becomes alive again. One must die to truly live, and His life was no exception.

He bowed His head and relinquished control, allowing darkness to wrap its arms around him, bathing Him. He did not resist as He was swallowed by death, falling into the blackness, engulfed by it peacefully, silently, like one drifting off to sleep.

Then suddenly, He was awake. Liquid light that He had always known but dearly missed was streaming over Him, washing over Him like water but not leaving Him wet. He soaked it in. His body healed. The darkness was gone. It was over.

He looked up and saw Him. He had not questioned the nearness but to see Him again brought such relief and comfort to His heart. Every struggle that He had been victorious over, every temptation that He had succeeded at resisting, every thought that had bombarded His mind as they do every human on earth, ceased. The tears dried and He knew they would never be needed again, but in that very moment tears began to fall again, this time out of sheer joy and awe. It was beyond words to be with The Eternal like this again.

Others were there. There was one man that seemed especially undone, the way one is when they do not deserve something but find themselves planted in the midst of uncountable blessings nonetheless. Jesus walked up to Him, placed His hand on the man's shoulder, and lifted him to his feet. He took the man's face in His hands, looked him in the eyes, then kissed him on the forehead.

"I told you that you that I would see you here." Lurching, the man wept. Christ simply held him. The songs wrapped around them from the many that were singing as Jesus walked with the man to the front, near the One encased in light. Jesus sat, and patted a throne next to Him, motioning the man to sit. The broken man sat, overwhelmed but not ashamed, just humbled and overjoyed to a degree that few have ever felt.

Jesus turned and looked upon The Eternal. The One wrapped in light was beaming back at Him. "Well done, good and faithful servant. I am so proud of you." The Father leaned over and wrapped His arms around His one and only Son. He had not held Him in what felt like a very long time. He had watched His Son be mistreated, beat, misunderstood, spit on, and finally, brutally killed. All He had wanted for so long was to simply hold Him. He had wanted to spare Him from all of the pain, but Christ had heroically chosen it. And while it broke The Eternal's heart to watch Jesus go through what He had, He understood why He chose it: For love. And they both knew it was the only way to right what had been wronged.

They stayed there for what could be said were years, enjoying one another, though it was only hours on earth.

After a particular celebration that had been unceasing for months, The Eternal turned to Jesus and with a smile on His face said, "It is time". Jesus knew what that meant; He had been waiting for this moment for thousands of years. He leapt up and headed out, descending.

The lack of light did not bother Him. It had not on earth either, but that does not mean that it is not wonderful to be back in it. He found them quickly, prisoners cut off and waiting, and told them the simple Truth. The decision was theirs. Many listened. Some did not.

He led them back along the path; a narrow walkway, one that only He knows. Even from a long distance away, He could feel waves of the Father's pride pulsating and resonating from where He sat. Pulse after pulse washed over them with a rhythm like the beat of a heart, consistent and warm. It was the heartbeat of heaven, and many in the group that accompanied Christ simply fell over when the waves gently washed over them. With each one Jesus patiently went over to them and helped them up to their feet, the inebriation of love being too strong for them to stand on their own. They were still weak in love, but quickly drinking so deeply of it that they would be like Him. One by one He helped escort each one back along the path that led home.

They were not even very near when they were met by The Eternal. From a distance they saw Home, and He sprung from the door, running towards the company with such joy and celebration that it was nothing short of terrifying. It wasn't that He was terrifying because He was going to do something terrible to them, but that His pursuit of them was so vehement, passionate, and determined that anything that got in His way would be defeated. For someone of such age, He was very quick. Each step was like an earthquake that shook you to the core, each blazing movement of His legs cut through the air like a sword. You could feel and hear Him coming. Then He was upon them, and with one fell swoop picked them up in His arms. He spun in joy, the way a father does when he picks up a child that they haven't seen for quite some time. It was at that moment that all of Heaven stopped and looked in awe because the Father began to weep. It suddenly became clear that while He did all of this for us, from the start to the end, He also did it because His own heart could not bare being away from His children. He made a way when we could not, and in doing so, ensured that His own heart would be whole once again.

The celebrations only got better, going from glorious to more glorious. With each saved soul it increased. And before they knew it, the three days had passed. All assumed positions from which to watch the Son return and take back that which was His.

He woke. Opening His eyes, He found Himself back in that odd experience of darkness. He was laying on stone. He smiled as His hands moved over his body and He found it healed and without holes and tears.

Something was nearby, someone familiar. He could feel and hear them. Then, with no warning, there was a shaking and light streamed into the small enclosure as the angel rolled the stone aside. He stood and walked out, alive.

Doing As He Did
(Acts 9:36-42)

Peter got out of bed and stumbled towards the door. His body was weary from all that had been happening and he had been on the verge of falling asleep prior to the knocking. Slightly irritated, he wondered to himself who could be knocking on his door at such an hour. They kept rapping incessantly on the door until he swung it open. Two men with concerned faces stood before him.

"Peter, please come at once!"

Peter got dressed and followed the men. They wove through dark alleys and through the city streets until they came upon a small house that had candles lit in the windows. The men motioned for Peter to go inside.

Upon his entry, Peter was greeted by a number of women, all engulfed in grief. The women began showing Peter robes and other clothing saying, "She was so skilled! It is a terrible thing that she is gone!"

Peter agreed: It was a terrible thing that Tabitha had died, but something about the way the women were treating the situation didn't sit right with him. While Peter grief was completely understandable, it wasn't necessarily helpful at the moment. Grief is the acceptance of something terrible happening, but faith, while acknowledging the terrible thing, does not accept the situation for what it is until Heaven's will has been affected. Peter knew that the faith he felt deep in his spirit would not easily mesh with the atmosphere of grief that had been created in the home, and he knew he needed to do something about it. He did not mean to offend anyone by asking them to leave, but he knew that if what his heart hoped for happened as he suspected it may, then grief would no longer be an issue. Grief has a way of telling a person in faith to give the one grieving something different than what they really want; their loved one back. Peter reminded himself that it was most loving to restore Tabitha to life.

Gently he said, "Ladies, thank you for being here. I can see how much you loved Tabitha. I loved her too. Could I ask something of you? Could I have some time alone in here to pray? I won't be long."

The women graciously agreed and backed out of the room. Peter closed the door behind them, then made his way to the back room where the body lay. He looked upon Tabitha. In all the time he had known her, he could not recall even one time when she wasn't doing some sort of act of service for someone else. She stayed busy, continually providing for the poor and selflessly looking after others. It was not okay that she had grown sick and died.

Peter fell to his knees in prayer. He knew he couldn't do what was in his heart, and the only way to see this happen was to connect to the One that could. He closed his eyes and began praying. Soon he was seeing pictures of Tabitha dancing in a field of flowers. A smile stretched across his face and his heart grew with even more faith because instead of assuming that the picture was reflective of her in heaven, he chose to believe that the picture was an indicator of what could be for Tabitha on earth. Jesus had not taught him or the others to think in terms of if someone that has died wants to come back to earth or not. Jesus had never told Peter or any of the other disciples to be concerned with the will of the dead, but to do as He told them, which was to raise the dead.

Peter knew that when we are more concerned with consorting with the dead than the King of Kings, the result is confusion and unbelief. "He is not the God of the dead, but of the living!" Peter thought.

It was time. He had seen it. Now he simply needed to call it into reality.

"Tabitha, get up!" He declared.

She opened her eyes. It had been so effortless that for a moment Peter wondered if everyone standing outside had simply mistaken her for being dead when really she was just sleeping.

Tabitha looked at Peter and sat up, surprised that he was there with her.

"Peter?"

"Yes. Here, take my hand." Peter reached out and pulled her to her feet. "One moment." He said.

He walked out into the front room and out the door, finding the women outside still teary-eyed and somber.

"Ladies, I have something to show you." He said. Leading them inside the home, Peter called out for Tabitha. She walked into the front room and the women gasped and ran to her.

The two men that had led Peter to the home came over to him, rejoicing. "We knew God would do it!" they exclaimed. Many heard about what had happened and as a result, many gave their lives to Jesus.

Gathering Around Paul
(Acts 14:19-20)

The last stone collided with Paul's skull. He saw it coming and didn't resist. There was a cracking sound, then everything went black.

Barnabas and the disciples had not known what to do or even what was happening. All they knew was that Paul had been suddenly pulled away from them and was no longer near them. They could see people gathered in a circle not far away, yelling, but a steady line of men were keeping them from moving forward.

The stoning had gone on and on. One would think that such an activity is over quickly, but something wicked happens in a person's heart as they engage in such a thing that makes them want to stretch it out for as long as possible. At first the mob simply wants to end the person's life, but once they see that the person isn't going anywhere due to a few solid hits, they pick smaller and smaller stones to throw so that the person really feels the punishment. They go from needing the person to die to needing the person to die slowly because the only way to truly satisfy a murderous spirit is to enjoy it by taking your time. Fangs give birth to fangs. Wickedness lends to more.

It must have been an inexperienced stone-thrower that had lobbed the jagged stone that finally caved in Paul's head. They stood around him, gloating, still on their religiously-inspired high. Then slowly, reality came back to them. Some suddenly felt appalled, guilt, and shame but the situation was what it was. It was done.

A man grabbed the bloody man's arms and began

awkwardly pulling Paul's body out of the area. A few followed him, sometimes helping, sometimes just walking and staring at what they had just done to this preacher. The crowd dispersed enough for Barnabas and the disciples to get through the mass of people that were intentionally keeping them from the place where Paul had been taken, and they saw the man dragging Paul out of the city. They followed.

As it set in what had happened, some of the disciples felt anger overtake them. Others were in shock.

The man finally dropped Paul on the ground outside the city and walked off. Barnabas and the disciples ran over to Paul and gathered around his broken body. Whether he was dead or not was not overtly clear; what was clear was that if he wasn't dead, he was so close to death that he may as well be.

They gathered around the body and began to pray. Soon a tangible peace descended upon them, heavy and pacifying. In many ways they ceased praying in the traditional sense, and shifted into the kind of prayer that has more to do with just enjoying the Presence of God.

Suddenly, Paul coughed. The group opened their eyes and saw that the blood that had covered most of his body was completely gone. His once caved skull was now restored, and the broken and bruised limbs were completely healed.

Laughter broke out. It was all so intense and ridiculously wonderful that laughter seemed like the only logical response. Paul stood up, dusted himself off, and they walked back into the city.

The Awakening of Eutychus
(Acts 20:9-12)

It was late, past midnight. His eyelids grew heavier and heavier until he could no longer fight their weight and succumbed to the gentleness of sleep. His body relaxed, then fell.

He had been seated in the window of a room on the third floor. Those present ran out of the room and downstairs to see if he was alright. Unfortunately, he was not. The fall had killed Eutychus, and many of those that rushed out to check on him stood there breathless, surprised that such a thing happened during church, of all places.

Paul calmly walked downstairs, listened to them tell him he was dead, then went over to the body and embraced him, laying upon him. Everyone nearby watched.

Paul knew those standing around him needed faith. He knew they were alarmed and being effected by the trauma of what had just happened. He knew they had their eyes fixed on the natural, so he simply declared the opposite of what was in front of him. "Do not be alarmed, he's alive!"

But he was not. Yet. Paul got up and went upstairs, broke bread, and ate. It was as though nothing bad had ever happened. Paul was seeing that which was not as though it was, and he was consciously choosing it. He was seeing that which would be as though it had already happened.

He continued speaking to the group, largely ignoring the issue of what had just happened. This offended some of the people there, but everything he was doing was full of faith and trust. His eating. His moving on and continuing to speak. His choice to not give the issue any more attention, it all was full of faith. Sometimes faith looks like folly to those in unbelief.

As a result, at some point between when Paul declared that the young man was alive and when Paul left in the morning, Eutychus did exactly as Paul had declared; He was alive again. The people took him home, greatly comforted by what God had done through Paul.

Witnessing Witnesses
(Rev. 11:11-13)

The two bodies had been laying out in the middle of the street for three days. Usually when someone dies, people gawk at the sprawled out body out of horror, but this time was different; people stared in delight. Everyone came, from near and far, to witness that witnesses had in fact, died. So many came that those with a entrepreneur bent quickly set up shop and began selling goods. Others, with more political stature and clout, effectively rigged up a series of walkways and booths so that people were forced to pay entry fees to see the glamor of the two bodies laid out.

When they died people rejoiced like their favorite sports team had won the championship. The parties continued unceasingly. After all, most of the hardship for quite some time was being associated with these two. You could step outside and hear the celebration from all sides in the city. It wasn't uncommon to have a gift mailed to you from someone you only remotely knew like it was Christmas season, simply because they were dead.

As the sun set on the third day, the masses began to head back to the various locations where they would partake in the many forms of debauchery that they were so accustomed to. As they left, their gloating was audible. One man said, "Not like your Christ, eh? They say he rose on the third day!" He spat on the body in front of him, then kicked the body in the side. "But not for you, half-wit! When you die nowadays, you stay dead, you hear? There be no such thing as resurrection!" A drunk man nearby chimed in, "True Harold, except what they do in Haiti. Right?" Harold looked at him, snapping out of the rage that he had worked himself into and coming back to reality, "Right! Too right! Come on, let's go. We can come back tomorrow!" The two walked off, sniggering.

The sun rose on the fourth day. The sun beat down on the people that waited their turn to see the decomposing corpses, many using handheld fans they had bought at a nearby stand to cool themselves.

Around noon, when the crowds were the largest, something happened. A fresh, cool wind blew through the crowded street. Those that had fans dropped them to their sides and pointed their faces upwards with eyes closed, taking in the momentary relief. You could hear the sigh of relief that went up from all sides, that is, until the first scream.

The woman had one hand on her cheek and the other was pointing in horror at the bodies on the ground. Everyone looked at her because of the sound she was making, then as though it was in slow motion, the whole crowd went from looking at her to looking at what she was pointing at.

It was unmistakable; they were stirring.

"No!" bellowed Harold. "It can't be! No god, please no!"

The two men stood to their feet. Gasps could be heard and Harold's begging prayer ceased. The men said nothing, just slowly turned as they looked at the people that were densely encircled around them. There was no escape, but neither looked concerned. Their eyes were electric, full of life and passion. They looked more alive than ever.

"Come up here" resounded from above. Everyone

heard it. It was impossible not to. And with that, the fog came. The day had been incredibly clear but nonetheless, fog had rolled in. It was so thick that Harold could not see his feet when he looked down. Chaos broke out as the people assumed that more tricks were being played on them. But just as they were about to trample each other in an attempt to leave, the fog began to lift. It did not leave as fog normally does, rolling out in the same way that it rolled in, but it literally lifted. It started at the ground and began moving vertically upwards, until the people could see what looked like the underside of a flat cloud rising above them.

Someone yelled, "They are gone!"

Another person somewhere else in the crowd responded, "They are using their witchcraft to levitate in the cloud! They are trying to escape! Get them! Do not let them get away!"

Men ran to nearby buildings and climbed the stairs in an attempt to get to the same elevation that the fog had rose to. Many succeeded, but did not know what to do once they ran out on the roof of the buildings because once again, they were encased in fog and could not see.

The cloud continued to rise. "They are getting away!" Harold screamed, clenching his fists and bearing his teeth in desperate anger and helpless frustration.

They were never seen from again.

ACKNOWLEDGEMENTS

Christine, I love you. Thank you for loving me. You are an amazing mother and I am grateful you chose me. You are beautiful and will always be my chai tea woman. I wouldn't trade you for the world.

Joshua, Jacob, and Lily, you are my daily dose of tangible joy. I love you more than words can describe. I see your mother in your face and hear God in your laughter. Love Jesus, no matter what; He will never fail you.

Mom, I couldn't ask for a better mother and grandmother. I love who you are. I know you want to get to dad but you have a long time left on this side; get used to it. You are my greatest hero.

Raleigh, I appreciate you more than you will ever know. Thank you for always being present and for doing life alongside me from a thousand miles away. You are a master at many things, but treating others as an equal when they are not may be your specialty. Whatever your do, you will never be paid enough. Over the years I have noticed that you have been a teacher and father figure to me, while somehow overshadowing those realities by being an even better friend. Succinctly, my dad's death left a void in my life that you have played a part to fill. Because of that, I know that my dad continually thanks the Father for you. You have shown me how to love well, fix things, raise kids, and to love God. I cannot recall even one time you have hurt my feelings or upset me. I still want to live in Hawaii next door to you as we enjoy No. 7, talk about God, fix cars our kids break, and start our own coffee shop. That may be what it takes for me to finally succeed at "Love your neighbor".

Jeremy, you are a master at relationship. I can't thank you enough for who you have been to me. Many times you have been the voice of God to me. I love how unoffendable you are and I deeply admire your relational loyalty. I am indebted to you in so many ways. I can't wait to see how God will weave our lives together in the future. You will counsel kings and priests.

Lyd, your consistency in loving me and those around you astounds me. You embody grace. You have been such a faithful friend, always there to talk, counsel, and affirm. Few have backed me as you have. You see me for who I am and affirm that even before I realize it. Thank you, I love you.

Daryl and Bob, in the current church climate, you are Hawaii to me. Thank you for trusting me and for valuing what God has put in me. Your affirmation has meant worlds to me. You and your wives are incredibly wise and I am honored to forerun life alongside you. Love you guys.

Jonathan, it has been a joy getting to know you. Thank you for being quick to laugh and for always being present in both relationship and work. Let's call in the school. By the way, your impressions are amazing.

Zack, Levi, Gabe, and Laz, thank you for being a safe place for me to unwind. You each make me laugh a lot. I love you guys. Triple digits is not impossible; I'm down.

Dustin, I love you. There is so much favor on you. Wealth will be yours; you couldn't avoid it if you tried. It will simply come to you. I still laugh every time I think about the time you burned your hand on that terrible coffee in the taxi on the way to speak in India. At least that man isn't deaf anymore! Thank you for being an awesome friend while many come and go.

Steven, you are having a little girl. You are doomed to have your heart melted daily. She will be beautiful. I wish we lived closer to each other. I still think you are one of the most anointed worship leaders I have ever heard, and if there was one person I could have serenade me, it would be you.

Clint, despite being incredibly busy, I always felt like you had time for me and my family. Thank you for being a safe place for us. We love Texas, but mainly just because y'all are there. I love you and loved being in Peru with you. What you will accomplish is far greater than you have imagined and I am excited to see what it will be. Space travel? Owning a planet? President? Only time will tell.

Teresa, thank you for being you. Your call in the Kingdom is so incredibly important. We are grateful for you and to you. You are family.

Big thank you to Marc and Lydia, Ken and Michelle, John and Evangeline, Tony and Rhonda, Jonathan and Rachel, Karen R., Dustin and Kit, Sylvie and Bob, Toni and Ted, Raleigh and Jenny, Bob and Lori, Daryl and Lynn, Chad and Mary, Bill and Beni, John and Lily, Sid and Melanie, Ron and Donna, Sam and Cherie, Brett and Julie, Abraham and Sheila, Michael and Sunshine, Brandon and Tracy, Richard and Rita, Glen and Kate, Earl and Jana, Brian and Cindy, Shannon and Michelle, Kris and Stacey, Martin and Brenda, Benji and Abbi, John and Linet, Tracy, Cindy and Greg, Timothy, Edwin and Marsha, Shawn K., Chris Evans, Ash and Katie, Pastor Scott, Ken and Michelle, Manju and Minoli, Adam and Katie, David K., Alvin Healing Rooms, Paul and Ginny, Kell B., Kevin and Allison, Kendall and Jessa,

Millian and Lyn, Mary D., Kristine DeMara, Jim and Maria, Bryan and Amy, Brea and Jill, Robert and Hannah, Gene and Lori, Clint and Melissa, Robert and Nicole, Kirby and Fi, Bruce Milne, Raj, Lauren P., Tim and Silvia, and last but not least…the almighty Sung. You have all sowed into our lives in countless ways and we are grateful, humbled, and blessed by you. We madly love each and every one of you!

TO THE READER

Nowadays, positive Amazon reviews are usually what decides the overall success of a book. If you enjoyed reading "The Dead Are Raised", would you mind giving it a stellar rating on Amazon? And for those of you that really want to go the extra mile, you can take a picture of the book and post it to your favorite social platform. This helps let others get blessed by the book as you did. Thank you, we are grateful!

How To Raise The Dead

Practical teachings on how to build your faith to a place where healing the sick and raising the dead actually become a tangible reality. Intimacy with Jesus, understanding righteousness, grasping the goodness of God, and other revelatory truths come to light through reading this book, enabling the reader to embrace faith that leads to "greater things you will do".

Stories of the Supernatural

Story after story of how Tyler found God in Walmart and other unlikely places. A high witch is saved and healed. Cripples walking. A whole tribe comes to the Lord. These are just a few of the stories you will read about in this bestselling book.

The Coming

Scythe is one of the many that is living in the last days. He serves in The Chosen, a group of people not cowering and fearful in the end times, but overcoming and victorious. They are the last remnant of what used to be. Or so they thought. A heretic that has recently arisen, claiming to have greater truths than what Scythe's people grasp. The Seers have sent Scythe to confront and convert this heretic, and the conclusions he comes to about The Eternal surprise him. Everything he thought he knew is shaken. Will Scythe's discoveries shake you as well? Our first fiction. Just read it.

The UnRedeemed

The second installment of our fiction series. This is the story of love's greatest triumph. This is the epic that all have lived through, and will live through. This is the ultimate story of redemption, wherein is declared, "O death, where is thy sting? O hell, where is thy victory?" Discover grace in its most just, pure form. Go with Scythe as he explores the realities of heaven and hell alongside Joshua in this sequel to "The Coming".

Invite Tyler

Want Tyler to come to your group, church, city-wide meeting, or conference? Email us at OneGlanceMinistries@gmail.com for inquiries.

School of Resurrection

Five sessions of resurrection testimonies, biblical teachings, mind-blowing revelation, and impartation. This two to three day conference is like no other. Those that go through the SOR are incredibly blessed, challenged, encouraged, comforted, and filled. This is a life changing handful of days and will take you and your fellowship to a new level of faith and revelation.

YouTube Channel

We have a youtube channel full of fun, faith-filled videos. Come hang out, subscribe, and enjoy. Search channels for One Glance.

India Trips

We lead teams to India in the winter months. Come with us. You will never be the same again. More info at OneGlance.org.

Establish a DRT in Your City

Our vision is to have a team of deadrasiers in every

city in the world, prepared and ready to raise the dead if the situation presents itself. It is time for the Church to not sit back and allow the enemy to steal, kill, and destroy but to step in with the authority of God and uproot the work of the devil with the love and power of God. If you want a DRT in your city, email us at TheDeadRaisingTeam@gmail.com to set up a School of Resurrection. We try to bring the training anywhere it is desired, yet ask that one or more church bodies are interested in order for it to take place. Work with those in your city, cast the vision, and bring Tyler out. Let's see the obituary page in the newspaper shrink!

ABOUT THE AUTHOR

Tyler grew up in church but never fully bought into Christianity until he went on a mission trip to Vancouver, Canada when he was seventeen years old. In the red light district of the city, Jesus appeared to Tyler while ministering to prostitutes. The encounter wrecked him in the best of ways and he fell in love with God for the first time that day, completely surrendering his life to Christ.

A few years later Tyler's father died in his arms and everything changed. Many things that Tyler had been taught in church over the years were questioned and compared to scripture. Starting back at square one, Tyler discovered the goodness of God in the midst of loss as he gave himself to long hours of worship and prayer. A big reason why Tyler carries the message of resurrection life is because he knows how it feels to have a loved one stolen. By giving his life to the message of Christ and Him being raised from the dead, Tyler hopes that that others are spared from the pain he went through. Tyler loves seeing the Church arise to Her call of imparting life and life abundant to a broken world.

Tyler and Christine were married in 2008 and now have three incredible children. They have been in full time ministry for almost a decade, working in Healing Rooms, speaking at conferences, leading trips to various nations, writing books, praying for the sick, directing Dead Raising Teams, and of course, playing way too much with their kids. Tyler became a best selling author in 2012 with "Stories of the Supernatural", but considers his best work to be his two fictions, "The Coming" and "The UnRedeemed".

When Tyler isn't traveling he enjoys roasting his own coffee, connecting with friends, marinating in God's love, and being with his family. He intends to live until Christ returns (2 Tim. 1:10), live in Hawaii someday, and leave a legacy on earth for generations to come.

PARTNER WITH US

Here are some of things that we do: We write awesome books (right?). We travel and break open new revelation in regions, planting teams that bring the Kingdom of God. We heal the sick and raise the dead. We lead mission teams to third world nations, preach the gospel to the unreached, love the poor, and establish community development programs that help provide the poor with work so they can sustain themselves. We direct Dead Raising Teams and facilitate resurrection prayer in cities all over the world. Soon we will be providing free medical clinics overseas. We co-lead our local Healing Room, and speak at conferences.

We do what we do full time. We know everyone is a full time minister of the gospel but for us the phrase "full time" means that we have chosen to focus on others before we focus on our own needs. In doing so, we have made a conscious choice to trust God to take care of our material needs while we prioritize other people ahead of ourselves. This means that if He doesn't come through, we don't eat. This is easier talked about than walked out, and it took even more faith to walk out once we had children.

Yet, due to the generosity of believers, we have been able to do full time ministry for nearly a decade and we never missed one meal. It blows our minds on a daily basis. We are so incredibly thankful and humbled by every time someone gives. Some people hear the Still Small Voice and respond in generosity, some people don't hear anything but give anyways just because they believe in what we are doing and who we are. We cannot overstate our gratitude to everyone that has ever partnered with us.

If you would like to partner with us, go to OneGlance.org for more information on how to be a monthly partner or give a one time gift. Giving is tax-deductible under our 501c3.

64193675R00170

Made in the USA
Charleston, SC
19 November 2016